CORE VALUES

Serving Christ's

Cause *with*

Effectiveness

and Excellence

D0926219

George O. Wood

with **Randy Hurst**

TABLE *of* CONTENTS

[PREFACE]

W HEN A NEW LEADER COMES TO OFFICE, people often speculate about where and how he will lead. George Wood didn't leave people wondering for long. Soon after he was elected general superintendent at the fifty-second General Council in 2007, he identified five core values that would determine the priorities of his administration.

During interviews for these chapters, it was clear that Dr. Wood does not view these core values as just ideals or ends in themselves. In acting upon these values, his desire is to build bridges—especially to nonbelievers, people of diverse cultures, and younger generations.

Bridges must be built to the spiritually lost. Most nonbelievers in our culture today will not be reached by merely being given a piece of printed literature, a video, or an invitation to church. Relationships with nonbelievers must be built through meaningful interaction centered on their interests and concerns. Bridges must be built not only with words, but also with deeds and caring acts that demonstrate sincere, compassionate love.

Other bridges are built interculturally. As the diversity of the Assemblies of God expands, the resulting vitality and synergy will enrich the spiritual life of our

Fellowship and maximize its outreach to the lost.

Dr. Wood clearly articulates his respect and love for his Pentecostal heritage. With a correlative enthusiasm, he seeks to build bridges to succeeding generations and pass on the truths, values, and commitment that compelled our Pentecostal forefathers.

A thoughtful perusal of the Fellowship's development clearly reveals our founders' commitment to these five core values. Dr. Wood emphasizes them with fresh expression and focus while presenting some new approaches to advancing our historic mission—the mission that the Holy Spirit led our early leaders to begin more than ninety years ago.

Dr. Wood compiled these five core values during a one-week period just after his election. However, the convictions that underlie these values were formed in his mind and heart over several decades of ministry.

Dr. Wood's path in life has uniquely prepared him for his present responsibility. He is transparent and frank about his regrets and concerns. The anecdotes and testimonies he shares illustrate the values he presents and affords the reader a clear perspective of his personal convictions.

As you read, be alert to other priorities that transcend the scope of a single core value. Interwoven throughout the chapters are a number of cogent emphases that apply to more than one value, such as church revitalization and the necessity of the Holy Spirit baptism for effective Christian life and service. Maximize the benefits of Dr. Wood's insights by taking time to contemplate the challenges he shares. Jot down applications to your ministry, your present circumstances, and your vision and hopes for the future.

In the coming months you will hear more about the five core values described in this book. They are not just ideals toward which the Fellowship should strive. Rather, they are priorities for action. They reflect the DNA of the Fellowship and set our course in following what matters most to our Lord—serving His cause with effectiveness and excellence.

—RANDY HURST
Assemblies of God Commissioner of Evangelism,
Communications Director of AG World Missions

'VE PERSONALLY KNOWN EVERY GENERAL SUPERINTENDENT SINCE E.S. WILLIAMS, with the exception of Wesley Steelberg, who served only a short time before he died. I am very conscious of those who have preceded me in this office. Having known these exemplary people, I find myself feeling like a Joshua in the wake of a Moses.

My personality is perhaps a little more like E.S. Williams'. He was very quiet in demeanor, not outwardly bombastic or charismatic. I could tell you stories of Brother Williams that provide a window into his character. He had a great heart for God and was a man of great wisdom. Some of my treasured possessions are handwritten letters from him to me when I was a young minister.

Ralph Riggs is a personal hero to me because Brother Riggs had a very sharp sense of what God wanted him to accomplish in the field of education—in Sunday School, lay education, ministerial education, and higher education. This Movement owes Ralph Riggs a great debt of gratitude because he laid the foundation for much of the AG's transition from an enclave mentality to become the kind of instrument this Fellowship is for God in the world. Evangel University has named its new administration building after Ralph Riggs. If anyone deserves that, he does.

The twenty-six-year tenure of Thomas F. Zimmerman followed Brother Riggs. I learned so much from Brother Zimmerman. He could have been president of General Motors or a U.S. senator. He had enormous ability. I remember as a young minister walking into his general superintendent's office and seeing very neatly ordered stacks of paper on his credenza. "Brother Zimmerman," I asked him, "with all that crosses your desk, how do you keep track of it?" He said, "George, I read something once and I decide what to do with it. If it's a policy paper I need to go over again, I'll do that on occasion. But I learned from Eisenhower that you handle a piece of paper once, decide what to do with it, and move on." Since that lesson from Brother Zimmerman, that's how I've handled paper.

Following Zimmerman, G. Raymond Carlson was a superintendent with a true pastor's heart. He was so greatly loved. God knew this Fellowship needed a pastor when we went through the Swaggart and Bakker crises. Brother Carlson had an impeccable godliness no one could challenge. G. Raymond Carlson was an anchor for this Movement during that very turbulent time. And even with those crises, the Assemblies of God grew during Brother Carlson's tenure.

What can I say about Thomas Trask and his great vision? So many AG ministries today are attributable to Brother Trask—the National Prayer Center, the Center for Leadership, the partnership with Convoy of Hope, the growth of AG Financial Services, and too many other accomplishments to list. His passion for Pentecost, his love for people, his wonderful way of relating to people and showing genuine affection with a holy kiss and a slap on the cheek—those are inimitable qualities.

I can't step into Thomas Trask's armor any more than David could step into Saul's. I'm more like my dad. My dad didn't display public affection at all, maybe because he grew up in a very dysfunctional home. In fact, when Dad was in a church service and the leader would ask people to join hands and pray, Dad would almost go ballistic. Dad didn't hold hands with his own wife, so why would he hold hands with a perfect stranger? I'm more reserved. That's just part of my DNA.

If God would answer a prayer for me, it would be that I might combine the gentleness of E.S. Williams, the strong sense of purpose and accomplishment of Ralph Riggs, the sagacity and diplomacy of Thomas F. Zimmerman, the godliness and pastoral example of a G. Raymond Carlson, and the passion for the Spirit and the business sense of Thomas Trask. If I could just get a dash of each of those, I'd be in good shape.

I didn't think I would be elected to this office. At the 2007 General Council in Indianapolis I realized my name was being tossed about, but I really was happy with whoever was elected and always envisioned "whoever" to be "someone besides me." I was content with my role as general secretary.

The afternoon I was elected, I was looking out across the expanse of the General Council delegates.

Who is able to lead this great host? I thought. And, of course, no one is humanly adequate to accomplish God's purposes. That is what is so wonderful about ministering in faith. I felt the Lord speak to me, *My yoke is easy and my burden is light. I want this yoke to fit well, so it can be a journey of joy. I know there will be hard things to face. But you have always enjoyed whatever you have done in ministry. Enjoy this too, and make it a journey of joy.*

Shortly after the election, people began asking me what I was going to do as general superintendent. Since I didn't think I would be elected, I deliberately had not focused on any such goals. In fact, going into General Council, I made a list of things I wanted to do if I were *not* elected. So, I really had a blank slate concerning the superintendency. But within a few days, I began concentrating on the hallmarks that might measure this administration. Working through those issues over the course of about a week, one thing and then another presented itself. When I had completed these five core values, I realized that just about everything this administration will be doing fits within one of them.

These values do not represent my opinion alone. Several friends whose spiritual judgment I value and trust participated in this process. Our e-mails flew back and forth as we worked, and I deeply value the sound advice and counsel from their spiritual eldership. Thanks to the prayerful support of many such friends, I feel extremely comfortable in my spirit about the ideas I want to share with you, and how I believe God will use them in the years ahead. I believe the following chapters represent what the Lord wants me and the executive leadership team to strive for, and I believe every church, pastor, and congregant in this Movement can be an invaluable partner with us.

Coming into the superintendent's office I have prayed for two things essentially—one, that God would give me wisdom and two, that I would have strength, not simply physical strength, but empowerment.

There is a difference in the Greek between *exousia*, which is authority, and *dunamis*, which is empowerment. When you look at the fifteenth and sixteenth presidents of the United States, both of them had authority but one of them exercised the authority and made a difference in our nation's history. James Buchanan and Abraham Lincoln held the same office, but Buchanan didn't do anything with it. Lincoln, on the other hand, used every ounce of his authority to guide this nation through the Civil War.

I would never want to hold an office for the sake of a position. I want to see God do something. His allowing me to serve in this capacity is a trust. That has been true throughout my life as a minister. Really, whatever position of ministry we are in—whether it is pastoring or district leadership or serving the General Council—we hold our position as a trust. The office of general superintendent is not mine; it is the Lord's. I occupy it as His steward. I must exercise the prudence of a trustee in the care of what God has given us.

The following core values summarize how I believe God would have me fulfill my position of stewardship.

There are some ideas here, if you read the whole book, that may impress you as deserving chapters in themselves. But these values are meant to undergird many other principles. I am not trying to replicate the stated threefold purpose of the AG or our sixteen foundational truths. I want to communicate the nuances of this administration and its commitment to furthering what the Assemblies of God is already about.

This administration in the eyes of this constituency will either be successful in doing these things or *not* successful. These stated values are benchmarks. We'll either carry them forward or we won't. If we fail to adequately make them a reality, then the constituency has the right to say, "You know, you guys really goofed. You didn't do what you set out to do."

This book shares my heart. I hope you will communicate your thoughts with me after you read it. We are going to do our dead level best to further these values. A terrific team of people here, throughout the country, and around the world have a similar heart to work for God. With His help, these values can take on new life in this Fellowship. What you are about to read is achievable. I hope you will join with me and with committed men and women across the Assemblies of God in implementing what I believe is God's vision for a twenty-first-century church.

CORE VALUE ONE

PASSIONATE PROCLAMATION

JESUS IS

OUR SAVIOR,

BAPTIZER,

HEALER, *and*

SOON-COMING

KING

ROM THE EARLIEST DAYS OF OUR FELLOWSHIP, the Assemblies of God has proclaimed Jesus Christ as Savior, Baptizer in the Spirit, Healer, and soon-coming King. Proclaiming Christ is the reason we exist. When we talk about the Holy Spirit baptism, when we talk about spiritual gifts, when we talk about fruit of the Spirit, when we talk about any other aspect of the Christian life—we are talking about means to an end. But the end, the reason we exist, is to passionately proclaim Jesus Christ.

I use the word "passionately" for good reason. You can make a proclamation without any enthusiasm, without any sense of urgency. A passionate proclamation conveys our whole heart; it connects the vitality of our lives with the words of our mouths.

"Passionate" is closely tied to "compassionate." In recent years we have discovered the importance of the ministry of compassion. The world is not open to a gospel we preach only within our church walls. They are looking for evidence we care about people. They are looking for the hands and feet of the gospel. And there must not be a dichotomy between the way we live and the way we profess.

A number of studies have shown that there is little difference between how Christians in general comport themselves in terms of their ethics and morality as compared to those who are not believers. That ought not to be. Every follower of Christ must proclaim a vital relationship with a risen Savior by deed as well as by word. If we undermine our words by our deeds, we have lost the authenticity and the credibility of the gospel.

Our passionate proclamation must know no boundaries of social class, community structure, geographic barrier, or political border. My parents were missionaries to China in the 1940s. I watched my mother and father live out the love of Christ with every ounce of their strength. And when that window of ministry opportunity closed, they devoted themselves just as fervently to the needs of the congregations they pastored in the United States.

A passionate proclamation was the order of the day in the Early Church. Such a life-driven gospel message propelled the reality of Jesus Christ from Jerusalem through Judea and Samaria and throughout the Mediterranean world. May the Assemblies of God in this century hold to that living proclamation as this Fellowship continues to proclaim Jesus Christ as Savior, Baptizer in the Spirit, Healer, and soon-coming King.

JESUS, OUR SAVIOR

I think of an unassuming sixteen-year-old girl who attended our church a couple of times. I'll call her Amy. Amy hung herself in her bedroom. I was called upon to serve at the funeral. I'll never forget that day.

Amy's suicide haunted me because I realized in

looking back that our congregation probably did not do enough when she came into our midst to really reach her. We had hundreds of people. Amy had been a calm face in the crowd. We didn't sense her despair.

She was going through a very distressing time in her life. I realized just how fragmented her life had become when I did the graveside service. At the end of that service I watched as Amy's family walked to their cars. The grandmother on her cane walked to her car. The mother on the arm of her latest boyfriend walked to her car. The father with his new wife walked to his car. The older sister, alone, walked to her car.

Four members of that nuclear family left that funeral and went their separate ways. I realized that Amy, in her final months, just got lost in the process. There was no one to love her, no one to care for her. And our church missed that opportunity.

That will always haunt me. To this day I wonder if we had proclaimed Jesus as Savior and Lord by word and deed, would we have lost that girl?

I think of another family related to a family in our church. I'll call them Jack and Sharon. They often went camping in the Joshua Tree National Monument desert. One weekend they took with them their three-year-old daughter Laura. Sharon was preparing the evening meal and called for Laura. Laura didn't answer. Sharon went to get Jack who was visiting people in nearby campsites. Jack thought Laura was with Sharon.

They began going from campsite to campsite calling for their daughter. Laura was nowhere to be found.

Other campers joined them. Within a single month, probably ten thousand Southern Californians had searched every square inch of that desert looking for Laura. To this day she has not been found.

Laura would be in her mid- to late-twenties today if she is alive. But she would not know her true identity. Her parents, however, know her true identity. There are a lot of people in this world who don't have a sense of being lost, but God knows they are lost. And the church must know they are lost—lost in the sense they are distant from God, ignorant of God, and unlike God.

The church cannot be passive about the lost. Look at the Parable of the Good Shepherd. Ask yourself what church wouldn't be satisfied if 99 percent of its community were in the fold. But the Good Shepherd drops everything to go after the 1 percent that is not in the fold.

And the reality is, what church wouldn't be satisfied if 50 percent of the community were in the fold, or even 10 percent? If we as a church don't share that passion Christ has for the lost, we have missed our reason for being. The lost are why Jesus came to this world. And we must remember that each of us is a beneficiary of His passion for lost souls. He came, seeking to save the lost. Those of us who have been rescued must in turn, by word and deed, proclaim that saving gospel to dying souls around us.

JESUS, OUR BAPTIZER

By word and deed we must proclaim Jesus is the Baptizer in the Holy Spirit. If there is a word that is a good synonym for the word "baptize," it is the word "overwhelm." The word *baptizo* in Greek always means to be immersed. And to be immersed in the Spirit, to be overwhelmed in the Spirit, is part of what this Fellowship has always been about.

Spirit baptism is all about empowerment to take the gospel to an unsaved world. You hear a lot about Spirit baptism, but you don't see much Spirit empowerment. There is a disconnect. Unfortunately, in some of our churches there is never even talk of Spirit baptism. That ought to alarm us. The Baptism is the special treasure of understanding and experience God has given us in order to take the gospel into the world.

If the younger generation does not see in the older generation a connection between Spirit baptism, Spirit empowerment, and Spirit fruitfulness, that new generation is going to turn the whole thing off. We must practice a full-orb view of spirituality and the work of the Spirit in our lives. If we only focus on initial experience and don't have substantial evidence, it's going to backfire on us.

I wrote an article sometime ago, a ministers letter, on the whole issue of substantial evidence. I see a lot of young people having problems with our Pentecostal distinctive because we in the older generation have focused so much on initial evidence and our young people are looking for substantial evidence of the Spirit's work. It's not a question of either/or, it's got to be both/and. The initial evidence is clear in the opening verses of Acts 2. But the substantial evidence is in Acts 2:42-47. That concluding passage presents the marks of a vibrant, Spirit-filled church.

In my early twenties as an associate pastor at Central Assembly in Springfield, Missouri, my responsibility included preaching most of the Sunday night services. One Sunday night I preached on the theme, "When do we receive the Holy Spirit?" I had never heard a message like this in all my growing up years in the Assemblies of God, but I answered with four things.

✦ We receive the Holy Spirit at conversion. We cannot say Jesus is Lord except by the Spirit. He, the Spirit, causes us to cry out, "Abba, Father." We're indwelled with the Spirit.

✦ We receive the Spirit in the baptism in the Spirit. In John 20:22, Jesus says we receive the Spirit at the point of salvation. Acts 1:8 and 2:4 declare that believers will receive power when the Holy Spirit is upon them. That's a dynamic experience. The Holy Spirit indwells us from conversion, but the empowerment of the Spirit comes with the Baptism.

✦ We continue to experience the Spirit's filling. In the Book of Acts, it keeps saying the believers were filled with the Spirit. Peter testifying before the Sanhedrin was filled with the Spirit. That suggests, as we go along, our life is somewhat like a balloon. We are expansible and the Spirit's gift is infinite. We are capable of receiving more, the Spirit is capable of giving more, and yesterday's filling will not be sufficient for today's issues.

✦ We will encounter the Spirit in a new dimension when we receive our glorified bodies. The same Spirit who raised Christ from the dead will also raise us. There is yet a work of the Spirit to be done at the end of this life.

When I concluded that sermon, sat down, and the altar call was over, I was shaking in my boots. Top Assemblies of God theologians and executives were in that audience. Mother Flower came to me and said, "George, Daddy Flower wants to talk to you." J. Roswell Flower was the first general secretary of the Assemblies of God and basically set up the Assemblies of God along its organizational structure. J. Roswell Flower had taught Pentecostal and Assemblies of God history for years, and had made that history as well.

I am in trouble now, I thought. *They're probably going to take my credentials.*

I walked over to Daddy Flower and there was a sparkle in his eyes.

"George," he said, "I just want to commend you and I wanted to tell you it's been a long time since I've heard a sermon like that. But that's how we preached it in the beginning."

JESUS, OUR HEALER

We must passionately proclaim Jesus as Healer. He not only heals our bodies, He also heals our emotions and our relationships. Malachi talks about the healing of generations from the hearts of the fathers toward the children and the hearts of the children toward the fathers.

A lot of healing is needed in this broken world. Not a Sunday goes by in our churches but there are people who are broken in spirit. Jesus came to heal, and the church ought to be a healing place. That is why conflict, argument, and division in the church are so devastating. When the saints are at odds with one another, it acts like a blockage in the heart, keeping the healthy life of Jesus from flowing.

But Jesus' ability to heal a broken heart must never be used as a theological cop-out to deny His ability to heal physically. The most compelling proofs of that truth in my life have come through my family. I'm probably a Christian today in part because of those healing miracles.

My sister went to Central Bible College in Springfield, Missouri, wearing thick lenses in her glasses. I believe she only had about 20 percent vision in one eye and 50 percent in the other. In the Assemblies of God of the 1940s and 1950s, people would pray for you to be healed if you wore eyeglasses. It was not taken casually.

Doris had had it with people praying for her. During a revival at CBC her freshman year, she was kneeling at the altar and she began to have a vision of Christ on the cross. A voice inside her said, *Doris, take off your glasses.* She ignored it. *Doris,* the prompting came again, *take off your glasses.*

Doris resisted. She had been prayed for so many times. But the vision of Christ on the cross persisted.

Doris, she sensed in her heart a third time, *take off your glasses.*

My sister reached up, took off her glasses, and threw them across the platform. But in her vision what she actually was doing was reaching her hand up to take blood from the cross. She put the blood on her eyes. When she came out of the vision she could see perfectly.

I was ten years old when Doris came home that Christmas from her first semester at Bible school. The change in her was absolutely phenomenal. It not only changed her eyes, but it changed her whole personality.

My dad was poisoned on the mission field. He was visiting a Tibetan tribe. Christianity was not welcome in the region, and Dad missed some critical warning signs of his danger. The chief received him enthusiastically and let him pass out gospel literature to his tribe, but Dad neglected to notice the chief had not extended to him the normal courtesy of a gift, which would always be a silk scarf. If you were extended a silk scarf, it was a symbol you were under your host's protection.

After Dad had passed out gospel literature, he was sitting in the chief's tent eating *zama*, a Tibetan concoction that looks a little like a Baby Ruth bar. You take some tea, put butter in the cup, and drink it. With the residue, you pour in some flour and mix it. The mixture looks and tastes like dirt, but it's vital to your relationship with your host. If you're an honored guest, you get more rancid butter. If you are less honored or somehow suspect, you get fresh butter. Dad got fresh butter.

After Dad was done the chief invited him to stay that night. But Dad began to sense something was wrong. He excused himself and traveled on. He had a Chinese evangelist with him. As they started riding away Dad began to get deathly sick. They made camp and Dad realized he had been poisoned. He started throwing up vile, green vomit. He became so sick that he tried to break the crystal of his watch to let my mother know what time he died. He didn't have the strength to break the crystal.

In the early morning hours, Mom was awakened back at their home and felt the urge of the Spirit to pray for my dad. Without knowing the reason, Mom prayed until the burden lifted in the early morning.

Several days later Dad came home. Mom would normally have him deloused before he came into the house. Dad would have a lot of lice on him because one of the side effects of the local belief in reincarnation was people would not kill lice for fear they were former relatives. That day Mom just brought Dad right on in.

"What happened to you?" she asked.

Dad explained what happened, the day it happened, and the time.

"That was the time I was awakened to pray for you," Mom told him.

There are a couple of footnotes to this story. The first took place in China. About a month after Dad's poisoning, those tribal people were in town to get supplies. Dad was in the marketplace and some of them saw him. They just were ashen when they approached Dad.

"We gave you poison enough to kill ten men," they said. "You must have a very strong God who protected you. We want to hear more about your God."

One of my memories as a child is that group of about thirty men periodically coming to town and camping in our courtyard for a day or two and becoming open to the gospel as a result.

Fast-forward thirty years and Dad was having stomach trouble. He went to one of the top gastrointestinal doctors in Southern California. The doctor operated and removed most of Dad's stomach.

"In all the years I've operated on people," the doctor told Dad after the surgery, "I've never seen a stomach like yours. You have hundreds of polyps, and none of them are cancerous. Normally, where there are more than a few polyps, there's going to be cancer. Did you ever have a shock to your system that would have ignited this?"

And Dad had a chance to witness to him about this experience in Tibet so many years ago. The doctor was amazed.

Often, when I'm talking about healing before an audience I'll ask for a show of hands of how many can give testimony that at one time or another they have been healed. It never ceases to amaze me the percentage of hands that go up.

We proclaim Jesus as Healer—Healer of body, mind, soul, and spirit.

JESUS, OUR SOON-COMING KING

All that Jesus is to us in this life only hints at what He will be to us throughout eternity. At the same time, everything He is doing among us in the here and now is vitally connected to what He wants to accomplish in those endless future ages. Followers of Christ must discern a balance between anticipating Jesus' return that heralds those future ages and living each day in the present to the fullest.

You often hear people who take an interest in prophecy trying to discern if this generation is truly the last before Jesus returns. I take a more expansive view of prophecy. I believe this is the last generation because it's the only generation I have. Whether the Lord comes or I die, for me this is the end of time, the last generation.

We need to live with the expectation that at any moment we can step out of the confines of this world, either through the Lord's return or through our home-going. We're stepping into eternity and we need to live in expectation of that transition. We need to make every decision in life with the next life in view.

I'm convinced the Bible teaches us to be prepared for Jesus' return and to look for signs of His coming, but many people in church circles have become burned out by all of the speculative scenarios and dates put forward for the Second Coming. When prophecy teachers try to relate the day's headlines to particular Bible verses and make specific claims about things that don't occur, we naturally get disenchanted. But it is a mistake to shelve the whole thing.

We need to put the date setting and the speculative scenarios aside and get to the core of the doctrine. At its core, the New Testament simply says, "Jesus *is* coming." It is an undeniable reality. It's as real as gravity.

When Jesus says in Revelation that He is coming quickly or soon, depending on the translation, it's helpful to go back to the Greek expression. The Greek word is really a measurement of speed at the point of the event. Jesus is promising us, "When I come, it will be all at once. It will be suddenly."

We need that sense of the imminence of our Lord's return. The Scriptures give us three perspectives to live by. One is the imminence. Jesus is certainly returning, and when He does it will be suddenly.

A second, and not very popular, scriptural perspective is the promise of persecution as we wait for the Lord's return. That may seem foreign to many Christians in the United States, but believers around the world can attest to persecution at the hands of oppressive government regimes and majority religions. We need to be faithful to Christ in order to receive the strength we need for all of life's adversities.

But there is a third perspective when we consider the Second Coming. We also have the Parable of the Talents. In that parable, Christ couched His return in the language of a master's long journey. As the servants in that parable demonstrated, we may have a normal lifetime to live.

I think it was Martin Luther who was asked, "What would you do if you knew the Lord was coming tomorrow?" He said, "I'd plant a tree today."

When I was twenty I wanted to go to seminary. Some of my friends said I should dismiss the idea. After all, "Jesus is coming soon." From their point of view, my going to seminary for a degree would waste three years I could be reaching others with the gospel. At first I had no good answer for them. But then I began to consider the Lord's own example. If Jesus waited until He was thirty to begin His ministry, I could wait until I was twenty-four.

I had an experience when I was in China as a young boy. Dad killed this one hen for our meal, and when he opened it, there was this whole conveyor belt of eggs that were in various stages of development. As a kid I never knew that there was a development process for eggs. An egg came out, and an egg is an egg. But looking in that hen, I saw there was tomorrow's egg and the next day's egg and the next day's after that. I just was amazed.

Years later I was sitting in a class at Fuller Seminary dealing with Jesus and how to define the Kingdom, the tension between the now and the not yet, and all these sorts of things. Suddenly the memory of that hen came to me. If Dad had let that hen live, tomorrow's egg would have developed and the egg after that.

When the Lord comes, He's going to see if there were any expectations in our hearts, any plans, any dreams, any visions of what He wanted to accomplish. When He opens up the record of our lives, He will not want to see an empty nest. God doesn't want us just sitting around in a cubicle somewhere waiting for His return. We must work until the Lord comes back. We must proclaim Jesus is King. Our Lord is going to wrap up human history, not someone with their finger on a launch button for a nuclear bomb somewhere. Christ is the Lord of history and He's going to bring that history to its glorious finale. In anticipation of that day, we must continue to serve Him faithfully and fervently. It all comes back to passionate proclamation.

I think of the Ephesian church in Revelation 2. Jesus commended the Ephesian believers for their hard work, for their testing false teachers. But Jesus didn't stop there. In many ways, the Ephesians demonstrated the ideal church. But there was one critical element lacking in their walk of faith—they had lost their passion. Jesus called on them to return to the love they had at first.

Each of us must heed that call. Each of us must remember our first love.

I think of a time when I was about eleven. I was riding in the car with Dad. I was sitting in the front passenger seat and it was into the evening hours. And in the joy and contentment of that moment, I felt compelled to sing. Growing up in a minister's home, gospel songs were the first to come to mind. And there I was, with the wind blowing through that window, belting out gospel songs at the top of my voice.

After awhile I looked over at Dad. I'll never forget his reaction. Dad was not an emotional person. But as he was driving and looking ahead at the road, I could discern tears coming down his face. I don't know that I ever saw my dad cry other than that time. But it was as if he sensed the purity and innocent love of that moment. He saw demonstrated the pure love of his son toward the Lord. And for a godly father there can be no greater satisfaction.

That's the passion Jesus is looking for in each of us today. That's the passion we must communicate to a dying world. That's the passion that will carry us into an eternity more wonderful than our fondest wishes.

STRATEGIC INVESTMENT

THE NEXT

GENERATION

IS *the* LIFELINE

OF THE

ASSEMBLIES

OF GOD

TAKE A LOOK AT OUR ANNUAL CHURCH MINISTRIES REPORT and you may be pleasantly surprised to discover that the U.S. Assemblies of God counts some 1.1 million young people under the age of twenty-five among our 2.8 million adherents. Many church organizations would be absolutely thrilled to have some 30 percent of their constituency that young. Our Fellowship is blessed with a new generation of believers poised to impact our world.

But are we doing everything we can to prepare them for that mission? Every year the Assemblies of God sees some sixty thousand young people graduate from high school. As they leave home and community for college and career, how many of them are holding to their spiritual foundations? Fewer than you or I want to admit. David du Plessis said, "God has no grandchildren." It has been observed that the church is always one generation away from extinction.

We must think strategically of what the Assemblies of God will become if Jesus tarries thirty, forty, or even more years down the road. We must lay a good foundation for this church to continue to thrive and prosper.

The Assemblies of God is the result of one of the longest-running revivals in church history. When you consider that in 1914 the Fellowship began with three hundred representatives gathering in Hot Springs, Arkansas, and today counts some 58 million adherents worldwide and 2.8 million in the United States, that speaks of incredible growth. In just the last fourteen years, more than 1.5 million people have been baptized in water in the U.S. church.

But how will we conserve that harvest? How will we evangelize and disciple the next generation? How will we help young men and women navigate the critical transitions from elementary, middle, and high school, and on to college and the work force? I believe four key lines of investment in their lives will make all the difference in their future.

And their future is our future.

INVEST IN LEADERSHIP

When I became pastor in Costa Mesa, it was a small church. The first thing we tried to do was to build a strong nursery. Most of the kids at the church then were toddlers. God blessed, the church grew, and near the end of my pastorate we had two hundred babies and toddlers in the nursery. We also counted about two hundred senior high kids, a lot of single adults and young married couples, and many older parishioners.

Our weakest area was junior high or middle school. We had perhaps twelve to fifteen kids in the junior high program. Somehow kids came out of our strong elementary program and just dropped out. They didn't want to come to church; they didn't want to be involved.

I went to the board. "There's a young man in our church who has just finished college and seems to have a real ability to win junior high kids," I said. "I'd like to bring him on. He's got an offer to teach public school, but he's willing to come on staff with the church for less money."

We had a philosophy in our church board that we never made a decision unless we were united. I sensed the board's reluctance.

"Would you let me appoint a committee to look at it?" I asked.

They agreed, and I lost no time in appointing three board members whose kids were in middle school. They came back to the board the next month with a report.

"Our own kids don't want to attend this church," they admitted. "They're bored. We have got to do something or we're going to lose our own kids."

Without knowing where the money was going to come from, we hired this young man as a junior high pastor. One year later, we had two hundred junior high kids.

I share that story to illustrate a missiological principle. Do we wait until a strong national church is in place before we send a missionary to a region? Of course not. We identify the need in a region and pull together the resources to send someone there to lead people into growth. But too often at the local church level we have reversed that. We staff a church for maintenance rather than for growth.

Young people need lots of loving care and attention. Some churches try to meet that need with lay ministry rather than paid staff. Sometimes that can work if youth sponsors are uniquely gifted. But a paid staff better enables lay ministry to grow in a church. A dedicated youth pastor will administer and grow ministry so more lay people can be involved.

We need leaders to guide our young people into spiritual growth. We also need young people to respond to God's call to spiritual leadership themselves. The Assemblies of God faces a potential shortage of ministers in the years ahead. Already, we are seeing an aging clergy. Increasingly when I visit our districts, I see more people receiving their fifty-year certificate for ministry than I see young people receiving their ordination.

Our districts need to proactively evaluate high school students, church by church, who have a call to ministry, who show promise of ability and giftedness for ministry. Districts need to find ways to connect with those young people while they are still in high school and begin offering some form of high school vocational ministry workshops. Some districts are already doing this. It needs to become a normative practice.

This can begin with something as simple as a weekend retreat for those who are considering vocational ministry. For example, the Louisiana District every year does a two- or three-day session for young people in their district—high school students who are sensing God may be calling them to vocational ministry. It's fabulous.

As such programs develop, districts and churches can provide scholarships for these young people. And when ministry majors graduate from AG schools, our districts need to find ways to integrate them into ministry settings. We have too many cases where a $30,000 school bill is walking out of Bible college marrying a $30,000 school bill. You can't face up to $60,000 of debt by going into a $20,000 a year youth pastor's position.

Do I have the solutions? Not yet. But we are a Pentecostal church; we depend upon the Holy Spirit to give us answers. We need His guidance to strategically invest in a new generation of leaders.

Our senior pastors should be mentoring the young ministers on their staffs or in their congregations. I hear horror stories of how staff are treated sometimes by senior pastors. Senior pastors must build relationships, not merely give job assignments. And relationships take time.

I think of Oak Grove Assembly of God here in Springfield. Pastor Ron Morein and wife Melissa have made it a priority to mentor young ministerial students from the Assemblies of God Theological Seminary, Central Bible College, and Evangel University. Every year a steady stream of ministerial students moves through their church. Melissa teaches a class on Sundays for women in ministry and talks about life as a minister's spouse. And that is only one example. Relationship building needs to become an established pattern in our churches.

INVEST IN CHURCH LIFE

Our churches need to put a floor under young people's feet. One of the temptations in youth ministry is to simply gather a crowd and fail to give young people sufficient flooring for their faith once they get away from that Christian crowd. You can always collect a crowd—

just bring in a Christian band or some hot speaker. But the discipleship component is critical.

Dr. Robert Frost was my zoology teacher at Evangel back in the 1950s and later became the charismatic author who wrote *Aglow With the Spirit* and other works. He and his wife, Ruth, would attend our church when they were not traveling in ministry. In the early days of that little A-frame church we had before it ever grew, he prayed this prayer on Sunday morning: "Lord, help them to lay foundations strong enough to bear the weight You will later place on them."

That should be what we're praying for our young people.

Those foundations must come from more than a weekly youth service. The pastor's preaching must appeal to young people as well—not put them to sleep. As a pastor, I kept in mind a mythical congregation consisting of a ten-year-old, a teenager, a young mother whose husband had just walked out on her for another woman, an older person facing health issues, and a skeptic from the local university doing a comparative religions study. With each sermon I would ask myself: *Would this interest a ten-year-old? Would it interest a teenager? Would it speak authentically to the skeptic? Would it address the hurt issues of the young mother who had been abandoned? And would it address the spiritual needs of the older person who was going through tough issues related to health?*

Over time, I lost that focus, until I received a wake-up call.

The principal of the Christian high school where

my kids were going called me in late August one year, and said, "My sophomore Bible teacher has just quit, and I need somebody to quickly sub for that Bible class this year. Would you come over and teach sophomore Bible for an hour, three days a week?"

My son was in the class. This was an opportunity no father should miss!

I had about thirty-five to forty kids in my class. They were as uninterested in what I was saying as the man in the moon. It was a disaster. I was having discipline problems. I'm usually very easygoing and even-tempered, but I found myself throwing kids out of class for just talking.

Then it hit me. The problem was me. I was ready to blame them, but I was the one failing to make the class interesting. I was using language that was more adult. I was using religious jargon and clichés. I wasn't telling compelling stories.

If pastors are concerned about how to connect with their junior high kids, I'd recommend they go to their youth group and just start talking to them. Get feedback. Get all your teenagers together and have an evaluation sheet. Ask them to note during the sermon what they thought was interesting and what didn't interest them. Reward them with a pizza bash or something for being cooperative.

When young people know you are interested in their opinion and you want them to help you, they will respond. I learned as pastor that people much more readily identify with my weaknesses than my successes. When I am vulnerable and say, "I need help. Would you help me here? This is something I'm trying to improve on," people absolutely rally. Paul said, "When I am weak, then I am strong." It's when we admit we need help that we get help.

Young people don't just want to be handed something; they want to be a part of making something. But too often we in the "established church" look at their efforts doubtfully. We need to begin recognizing the wealth of gifts our young people have to offer, and open ourselves to viewing ministry through their eyes.

When I have studied the emerging Church in Scripture I've given a lot of attention to two models—the Jerusalem church and the Antioch church, both powerful churches.

The Jerusalem church had great growth. It had great spiritual vitality and experience in the Holy Spirit. It had miracles, signs, and wonders. But it also had a very well-defined cultural motif. The Jerusalem church did not change rapidly. Around A.D. 58 when Paul arrived in Jerusalem, they were still doing animal sacrifices. They asked Paul to sponsor four men who were under a vow. At least twenty-five years after the resurrection of the Lord, these believers were still involved in temple ritual. There was a strong conservative influence in the church that was concerned about circumcision and kosher and nonkosher food laws. And yet that church was dynamically reaching people within that culture.

At Antioch, different leaders, such as Barnabas, Paul, Simon of Niger, Manean, and Lucius the Cyrene, were reaching the Gentiles. The believers were first called Christians at Antioch. They were getting people's attention. There were different cultural customs. Believers would not have a problem eating a cheeseburger in Antioch. In Jerusalem they would have thrown a fit at eating a cheeseburger because it's not kosher. You don't eat a meat product and a dairy product at the same time. The Antioch believers were not hung up on issues of circumcision. Very important in this equation, they spoke the language of the culture they were reaching with the gospel. They spoke Greek at Antioch.

Bring this illustration into the twenty-first century, and you see models for two generations in the Assemblies of God. We need to recognize that just as two vital New Testament churches were widely different from each other but had the same doctrine and the same Spirit working within them, the older generation in the Assemblies of God needs to be able to say to the younger generation, "You are free to use the models that effectively reach your culture and we are going to affirm you."

I don't care how you do church as long as people are getting saved, baptized in the Spirit, called into ministry, healed, delivered, effectively serving Christ, reaching the lost, and discipling people. It's end results we need to be looking at, not means. We need to stop being hung up on means and get to end results.

INVEST IN EDUCATION

National studies indicate that evangelical churches lose 50-70 percent of their young people who go to a nonevangelical college. Evangelical schools, however, lose only about 5 percent. I want to speak very directly on this, because this is my concern.

We receive letters at the national office from pastors saying, "I sent my daughter to that school, and I'll never send another child to an Assemblies of God school because of what happened to my kid."

I understand that, and I bleed for parents. I had a child who for a while went astray after leaving an Assemblies of God school. But, you cannot expect our schools to be perfect, and they don't have perfect kids. Probably 40 percent of the students matriculating into an Assemblies of God college are from broken homes. Quite frankly, many of our colleges have higher standards for deportment than the homes and even the local church youth groups that many of those young people come from.

You cannot decry a beneficial system on the strength of isolated mistakes.

Why has the Assemblies of God been so successful in its international growth? Certainly, first of all, through the ministry of the Holy Spirit. But partnered with that Pentecostal distinctive, our educational philosophy has focused on preparing men and women for ministry around the world. We have poured massive percentages of our foreign missionary dollars into Bible schools, seminaries, and graduate schools around the world. Education represents the biggest proportionate expenditure of missions personnel money, bar none. We must recognize the strength of education's role in our international growth and apply it domestically.

Currently, of our sixty thousand high school seniors each year only about twenty-seven hundred are entering one of our nineteen endorsed schools. That's a little over

4 percent. Parents say AG schools are too expensive. But there are several ways of looking at this. Families with a small level of income can qualify for grants and loans that would make an AG school accessible. Those who have an average to upper income and are having difficulty with the price of the school often don't think anything about taking a cruise, a vacation, or a fishing trip. Those funds could be redirected in the short term.

We must make our schools a matter of priority. Either our young people are important or they are not. You have to measure worth versus cost. If you simply evaluate something by its cost and not by its worth, you are using the wrong measurement.

Our churches need to reevaluate their approach to our schools. As I travel, I'm in a different church almost every Sunday. I regularly commend churches for their heart for U.S. and World Missions. I see church bulletin boards covered with certificates of their support to various missionaries around the world. But then I observe just a token offering for one of our AG colleges. There is a more strategic approach a church can take to its investment in missions and ministry.

As a pastor, I determined we would give approximately 15-20 percent of our total giving outside the church toward our colleges. We gave $500,000 a year to World Missions in my last year of pastoring. Out of that $500,000, approximately $75,000 went to Christian education because it represented a strategic investment. How are we going to have next generation missionaries? Where are we going to find them?

On the home front, we're talking about planting thousands of churches in the Assemblies of God in the next few years. Where are we going to get those church planters? Where are we going to get the next generation of pastors, staff members, laity, and the like, if we don't strategically invest in our schools? Assemblies of God colleges are the power plants of production for the workforce that is going to be in the kingdom of God in just a very few years. Our churches must ramp up their support for Christian higher education to a level commensurate with how U.S. Missions and even World Missions are being supported.

I am not calling for a reduction in giving to our missions arms. We have the resources to radically increase our support for our schools without diminishing our support to missions at all. Our people will rally to a challenge. This church, for example, is great at compassion ministries in times of crisis. We gave eight million dollars for the 2004 tsunami in Asia; we gave between seven and eight million dollars for Hurricane Katrina relief in 2005.

But we currently give tiddleywinks in comparison to the most important task of this church—preparing the next generation for ministry.

Do I believe in compassion ministries? Absolutely. Should we be giving millions of dollars to compassion ministries? Absolutely. But we need to teach our people to not only give with their heart, we need to teach them to give with their head. And the fact is, we have got to make a strategic investment in this harvest; we have got to be more intentional in our churches about raising the level of support for Assemblies of God higher education.

I am a product of a generation before me that strategically invested in Assemblies of God higher education. I went to Evangel College. When you look at the history of Evangel, this Movement in the 1930s and 1940s clashed repeatedly over the idea of developing a college that focused on the laity rather than the clergy. It took leaders like General Superintendent Ralph Riggs, one of my personal heroes, to go against the crowd and do what was right. He believed in this concept of preparing young people for godly service in all walks of life. He believed it with all of his heart.

I am a debtor to people like Ralph Riggs and Evangel President J. Robert Ashcroft who said there is a need for this kind of school in the Assemblies of God. They strategically invested in the next generation. I had the privilege of being mentored by J. Robert Ashcroft. I attended Evangel when he was college president and later I was campus pastor under his leadership.

These people had a sense that what they did with young people was going to shape the context, the nature, of the church in the next generation. If they did not pay attention to the next generation, our Fellowship was soon going to be in trouble. That truth never changes.

INVEST IN RELATIONSHIP

I went through the Pauline epistles a few months ago and jotted down the names of all the people associated with Paul in ministry. I found more than sixty names. And I noticed two things: Paul did not refer to them in derogatory terms, and he made a point of avoiding hierarchical terms. These people were Paul's "fellow laborers."

Yes, there is hierarchy in any organization; there is structure. But the church is not a corporation. It is the living community of Jesus Christ, and we are bonded first of all by our relationships before we are bonded by structure. If ministry doesn't flow out of relationship, ministry is not going to happen.

One thing this Fellowship is facing with younger ministers is that they are less enamored with ecclesiastical structures, rules, and regulations. I have tried to encourage district offices in the fourteen years I have served as general secretary to let the credentialing process not just be a gate we guard, but a welcoming mat we offer.

Younger people tend to ask more questions. We cannot let that be viewed as being rebellious or disrespectful. We need to be mature enough to take a punch, so to speak, and if young people have hard questions— whether doctrinal, philosophical, or organizational—we cannot be defensive about that.

When I was a young minister, I'm sure I irritated the life out of some people. I was always asking and challenging. In fact, I just wrote my former district superintendent Bill Robertson recently. He sent me a nice letter of congratulations when I took office. I thanked Bill for putting up with me. I told him I knew I caused him many a headache on a district council floor and even personally. Yet he was always kind to me. I thanked him for that. We need that kind of inclusive attitude toward our younger ministers.

This generation doesn't want to wait around, and it's the best and brightest generation we've ever had. We have got to do our dead level best to retain this generation and expand. I'm going to be off the scene in thirty years if Jesus doesn't return before then. The young ministers coming up in our Fellowship are going to be around a lot longer than I am. They have got to have a hand in shaping this church.

In one sense, our older generation has a parental responsibility toward the next generation. As spiritual "parents," it is not our job to force young people into a mold. It is our job to motivate them to become all that Christ would have them to become.

Our son and daughter went to a nondenominational Christian high school. One of the teachers got very involved in an intellectual approach to some doctrinal issues I was uncomfortable with. My son, who is very bright, was becoming enamored with this. I wanted to encourage his theological curiosity; I did not want him to become an intellectual divorced from reality and practicality.

I came up with a simple plan. "George," I told him, "if you will read books about great Christian leaders and missionaries and write me a two-page report on that book, I'll give you $2 for every book report I receive."

Soon he was reading books out his ear, and I could hardly keep him supplied with books. He's in the pastorate today and has a great heart for God, a great heart for missions, and has balanced his tremendous intellectual skills with terrific emotional, spiritual, practical, and relational skills.

Every Tuesday morning my daughter calls me. "Dad," she asks, "what do you need for me to pray with you about this week?" She's my prayer partner, a strategic prayer partner.

Those relationships don't happen unless you build trust. As a parent you have got to spend time with your kids; you have got to nurture them. You must hold them up in prayer and continue to love them as they struggle through difficult seasons in life. And the same principles apply to the next generation in this Fellowship.

If we are going to win and spiritually nurture a new generation, if we are going to raise up young men and women to partner with us in reaching a lost world, the old adage holds true—honey is much better than vinegar. We will never attract young and vibrant Christians into our pulpits if we are seeking to repress anything in them that does not quite jell with our established sensibilities.

But if we will commit to doing all things in love, and if we will commit to recognizing and sacrificially supporting the gifts with which God has endowed the emerging Assemblies of God, I see an amazing future for this church.

The choice is ours.

VIGOROUS PLANTING

ESTABLISHING

NEW CHURCHES

MUST BECOME

this FELLOWSHIP'S

PRIORITY

W E'VE ALL HEARD OUR SHARE OF "GOOD NEWS/BAD NEWS" SCENARIOS. It's only natural we prefer hearing the good news first and downplaying the bad news.

Here is genuinely good news: The U.S. Assemblies of God is planting, on average, 275 churches a year. That works out to a new church every 1.3 days.

Here is the bad news: The U.S. Assemblies of God is closing, on average, nearly 275 churches a year. There is no avoiding or downplaying the reality that our Fellowship has barely grown for several years. This must change. If the Assemblies of God is to grow, we must focus on church revitalization as well as church planting.

Church planting is the most effective means for evangelization. New churches, by their very nature, have to grow to exist. People are motivated to get out and reach the lost. New converts more effectively reach other new converts because they still have a lot of non-Christian friends. When you plant a church in a community, you have a wonderful opportunity to impact that region with the gospel.

I will outline the need for more AG churches in our nation. Then I want to offer examples of just two church plants and the impact those churches have had on our world.

WE MUST REACH
UNCHURCHED AMERICA

Our AG Church Ministries Division reports there are 25,150 U.S. communities that can be identified demographically. The Assemblies of God has no churches in 18,742, or 74.5 percent, of those places. There is no AG church in three-fourths of America's identifiable communities.

Among the total U.S. communities, 18,969 are home to five thousand or fewer people. Of those, we have no AG churches in 15,934. That is 84 percent. I realize we put a lot of emphasis upon urban church planting, but there is room for a lot of churches in small towns and rural America.

At the opposite end of the spectrum, 230 U.S. communities have between one hundred thousand and five hundred thousand people. We have churches in all but six of those cities. That sounds like a solid track record until you stop and think about it—six cities with six-figure populations without a single AG congregation.

There are thirty-one cities and communities of more than five hundred thousand people, and there are AG churches in all of those. But in many of those places there is only one AG church, or just a few small churches. That level of penetration does not significantly impact a city.

I love the term "churches of influence." Churches of influence impact their community. Recently, I heard of a church in a town of one thousand with a congregation of more than one hundred people. That is a church of influence—they represent 10 percent of the town. That kind of critical mass within a population can effectively communicate the gospel to the other 90 percent.

Church planting is going to be front and center in my service to this Fellowship. For some years the Church Planting Department has been a vital part of U.S. Missions. A new entity, our Church Multiplication Network, will come directly under my office. U.S. Missions will continue to select and support U.S. missionaries who are church planters, but everything else related to church planting is going to come directly under the general superintendent's office as a primary focus. If church planting is one of our strategic values and goals, it cannot be simply a department in a division. It must be front and center.

The MX9 project is one recent church planting emphasis. Under that banner, we hope to have one thousand new churches either on the drawing board or planted by 2009. But it is hard to visualize one thousand churches. So I want to consider in detail just two churches—two churches from our early history that are leaving twenty-first-century imprints on lives around the world.

ONE CHURCH, ONE FAMILY, ONE CHAIN OF GRACE

In 1994, I had the privilege of preaching the eightieth anniversary of First Assembly of God in Jeanette, Pennsylvania, pastored by Martin Koss. I knew a good bit of the history of that church even though I had never been there.

In 1914, the year the Assemblies of God was founded, a young preacher, single and twenty-four years of age, felt called of God to start a church in Jeanette. Ben Mahan had no money; he had no organization behind him. But he felt called. Lacking any resources, he went to Jeanette and took his position on the sidewalk of Clay Avenue, the main street of town, on Saturday night and set up an impromptu street meeting.

Those were the days when people shopped in the downtowns of America. You didn't have malls and extensive tracts of private property where they could boot you off for street preaching. (Sidewalks are still public forums under the interpretations of the First Amendment, so you can still preach on a sidewalk.) Ben Mahan preached on a sidewalk on Saturday nights. A lot of people would cross to the other side of the street to avoid him. Others, including a few drunks, would mock him. But a few people stopped and listened. People began to get saved.

Within a short period of time, Mahan had a group of people asking for a regular place to meet on Sunday. They rented the second floor above the butcher shop on Clay Avenue, and the church continued to grow. The Presbyterian church on Clay Avenue came up for sale in 1924 when that congregation built a new church. Mahan and his families scraped together enough money to buy that building. Soon they were one of the strongest churches in the Assemblies of God—sending missionaries and gathering about four hundred people in their services. This was a megachurch in the mid-1920s.

In that same town in 1910, four years before Ben Mahan arrived, a couple named John and Clara struggled to raise four children. John, a fireman in his early forties, died of a heart attack. Clara was widowed with four children—a girl, 6; a girl, 4; a boy, 2; and a girl, 2 weeks old. Having no vocational skills, no Social Security, no social safety network, she tried to keep her family together. She took in washing and ironing, whatever job she could get her hands on to take care of her children.

Several years after John died, Clara met a widower. He had six children. They married and had a blended family of ten children under sixteen years of age. Too late, Clara discovered her new husband drank and was very physically and verbally abusive. And he hated Clara's son.

When that boy was in the fifth grade, the stepfather put him to work in a glass factory. Jeanette had six glass factories and was the leading glass production center in the country. The boy worked the 3 to 11 shift. He had to take fifth grade twice because when he went to school, his teacher saw how tired he was and would let him sleep in the closet.

When the boy was in the eighth grade, his stepfather pulled him out of school permanently and put him to work in the glass factory six days a week. By the time that boy was sixteen, he was headed to hell in a handbasket. He was rebellious, he was smoking and cursing, he was running with the wrong crowd. If there had been gangs in Jeanette, he would have been in one.

Several years before, Clara had come into the church on Clay Avenue and accepted Christ as her Savior. One by one, her three daughters had come to the Lord. Her husband and his children would have nothing to do with the church. But Clara and her girls had come to Jesus.

Clara tried to get her son to come, and he always refused. One Sunday she asked if he would at least walk her to church. He gave in. When they reached the church, he would have stood outside, but Clara kept urging him to come in with her, and he finally agreed. He sat on the back row.

Ben Mahan had been pastor now for ten years and was married. He preached to his recently relocated congregation and gave the altar call. And that young man on the back row walked down the aisle, knelt at the altar, and gave his life to Christ. Two weeks later, at that same altar, he received the baptism in the Holy Spirit and was called to the mission field to be a missionary to China.

And of course, I know that story because that young man was my dad.

When First Assembly in Jeanette invited me to their eightieth anniversary in 1994, it was the first time I had ever visited the church. They had a new building, but the old building still stood on Clay Avenue. My sister was with me. We had seen pictures of the inside of the old church and wanted to visit it. An elderly gentleman let us in. The church is a black Baptist congregation today.

My sister and I sat in the back row. I don't know if it was exactly where Dad had sat, but the pews were the same as in the pictures we had seen. We sat and talked a long time. Then I suggested we walk down the aisle and retake the walk Dad took when he was sixteen. As we started toward the front, I began sobbing. It had never struck me before that when my dad walked that aisle not only did his life change, but the life of everyone following him changed as well.

Is church planting important? Did Ben Mahan make a difference when he obeyed God and began preaching on Jeanette's sidewalks in 1914?

I have counted the generations coming down from Mom and Dad. Mom and Dad had three children, and there are forty-three people in our extended family today, thirty-nine of whom are actively serving Christ. We trust the other four are on their way back.

Today in northwest China there is a church of fifteen thousand people planted as a result of my parents' efforts. There's a church in Ravenna, Ohio, that was planted. The church in Traverse City, Michigan, was planted.

All of those people are a product of Ben Mahan. I am a product of Ben Mahan. I never met Ben Mahan. He later pastored in Washington, D.C., and he died many years ago. But I am the beneficiary of his church planting efforts. Because Ben Mahan listened to God and went to Jeanette in 1924 and preached on the streets, I and a host of families around the world owe him many thanks we can only share with him in eternity.

What comes out of church planting is not buildings; it's people. Church planting is all about people.

WITH FAITHFULNESS, THERE IS NO FAILURE

I cannot neglect to mention what would appear to be my parents' failed church plant in Jeffersonville, Indiana. Jeffersonville is across the Ohio River from Louisville, Kentucky. The year was 1954.

My parents had been home from the mission field about five years. They had planted churches in Michigan and Ohio, all the while hoping China would reopen. They were out of a church and could not seem to get a tryout anywhere. Even their evangelistic meetings had dried up.

From my parents' perspective, this many closed doors could only mean God wanted them to plant another church. The Indiana District let them know about the need in Jeffersonville, and also mentioned a suburb of Indianapolis that needed a church.

Dad selected Jeffersonville. He found a small building for sale for about $11,000. It would seat about one hundred people and had an apartment in the back. Dad and Mom had $1,000 to their name. They could get that property for $1,000 down and then make the payments.

Mom and Dad decided before they signed the papers, they would look at the Indianapolis suburb. With no extra money, they planned to drive across state all night rather than stay in a motel. Those were the days of two-lane roads and little motels by the side of the road.

I was thirteen, the last child left at home, and I was sleeping in the backseat when Dad began to get very ill.

He would stop the car to throw up, get back in the car, drive on, then stop and throw up again.

He finally said to Mom, "I think I'm going to die. If you can find a motel for $4, we'll stay the night so I don't have to drive anymore."

I was very frightened. Mom did not know how to drive. They had no money to go to the hospital. The first two or three motels were $6, which was beyond Dad's decree. They finally found a motel for $4. When we got up in the morning, Dad was well.

"You know," he said, "the Lord must not want me to go to Indianapolis. We're going back to Jeffersonville to buy that place."

Back in Jeffersonville, Dad took a job across the river in Louisville packing and crating heavy cargo. Summertime in the Ohio River valley brought 100-degree temperatures and 100 percent humidity. We had no air conditioning. Dad would come home about 4 in the afternoon and lie down on the floor exhausted. Mom would put a little circular fan by his head. He would lie there for an hour and a half or so. Mom would fix supper. After we ate, Dad and Mom would go calling door-to-door, inviting people to church.

To supplement the family income, Mom took an Avon route. She had not done secular work since leaving a bank to become a missionary at the age of twenty-six. Those were the days when most Assemblies of God women did not wear cosmetics. Mom would come home with that Avon bag slung over her shoulder and I would say, "Mom, have you been pushing that lipstick again?"

"No, Georgie," she would reply very defensively, "I did not push lipstick. If people ask for it, I sell it. But Avon has many other fine products."

After Mom and Dad died, one of the things I got from Mom was a little pin I would wear on my lapel—"Avon Highest Honor." It was her sales pin award for selling Avon product.

Over the next two years I was baptized in water and took on my first "ministry." My job was to teach the four- and five-year-olds' Sunday School class. We had a one-room Sunday School. There were four classes in the sanctuary and there were benches. We flipped the next-to-the-last bench so my class was in the back right corner. My job was to keep those kids quiet so the other classes could function. I had a little shoebox with stick-up flannelgraph figures inside. If the children were good, I passed the shoebox around and they could look in and see the Bible characters in three-dimensional form. (Obviously, this was before MTV and video games.)

I had a paper route and essentially provided all my own clothing and food. Everyone in our family had to work because the income was so meager. At the end of two years in Jeffersonville, Dad's health broke and he turned the church over to the district. The district put someone in there briefly, but they couldn't make it grow. All we ever had was perhaps twenty-five to thirty kids and a few adults, most of whom were on welfare and couldn't pay tithes. The district sold the church to an independent Pentecostal woman pastor.

My parents never talked about Jeffersonville the

rest of their lives. They perceived it as their big failure.

I preached in Cincinnati, Ohio, in the late 1980s after my parents had died. I was only 120 miles from Jeffersonville, and I had not been back since I was fifteen. I rented a car and eventually found myself at the corner of Chestnut and Graham where the old church building stood. It was no longer there.

I got out and started walking around the block. I was sobbing. I don't think I've ever cried harder in my life. I didn't cry that much at my parents' funerals. I was just a basket case emotionally.

"Lord," I prayed, "my parents worked hard here and there's nothing to show for it. It's not fair."

I felt the Holy Spirit speak to my heart in a quiet way, but with a very strong rebuke.

George, you know better than that. A church is not a building. A church is people. Weren't you baptized in this church? Didn't you begin your ministry in this church? How can you say the church doesn't exist anymore when you exist and you're the church? You don't know who else your parents touched in this place who are serving Me today. Don't tell Me the church doesn't exist.

I continued to tell that story in my travels. In 2002, someone told me about a very strong Pentecostal church in Jeffersonville pastored by an elderly woman. I did some research, found her address, and wrote her. That began a four-year correspondence that culminated in October 2006 in my going to Jeffersonville.

Berniece Hicks is eighty-eight years of age. She is the one who bought the church. The church now has three thousand people. I have never been treated so royally in my life as when I visited Berniece Hicks and the Christ Gospel International Church in Jeffersonville. She honored my parents posthumously and honored me. I went back with my wife and my brother and sister and their spouses six months later. Again she treated us like we were royalty. She wants me to make an annual visit.

Besides the church in Jeffersonville, Sister Hicks and her congregation have started two thousand churches overseas. She has churches throughout Latin America and India. She speaks at huge conferences. She was just in Mexico City to speak to twenty-five thousand people there. She is a phenomenal woman of God, the church is a phenomenal church planting congregation, and all of this came out of a ministry my parents perceived as one in ruins.

Dad and Mom were just foot soldiers in the Kingdom. They worked with all their might at whatever they believed God would have them to do. Dad always wished he had had better training. He only had an eighth-grade education; the rest he did by correspondence. He pushed me so hard in education because he felt he could have done more had he been more capable.

My parents' dogged determination to serve the Lord left a deep mark on me. As I look across the landscape of the Assemblies of God and realize a third of our churches are under fifty in attendance and another third of our churches are between fifty and one hundred, I know from experience those churches and the ministers who pastor those churches are accomplishing great things for the Lord. They are drilling deeply into people's lives. We ought never to write people off on the basis of small numbers attached to their ministry.

Some today would have written off my parents as failures in ministry. They never pastored large churches. They were never in the spotlight. They didn't speak at district councils. They were just foot soldiers in the Kingdom. But their work—the Holy Spirit's work, in reality—remains.

Mother always used to say to me, "Georgie, when we stand before God, He will not ask us if we've been successful, but if we've been faithful."

That was her watchword. That was her motto. And I think she was right.

PARTNERS WITH THE SPIRIT WILL CARRY THE MANDATE FORWARD

Vigorously planting new churches is a continuity of Brother Trask's emphasis that every church should be a parent or a partner in church planting. We must strategically plant new churches. We must recognize no existing church or ministry has a fiefdom or a territory. We must work together to see churches begin filling the thousands of communities we have yet to reach.

One of the most successful church plants I have ever seen was in Fresno, California, years ago when Dave Gable pastored Full Gospel Tabernacle, an historic Assemblies of God downtown church. Another AG church started in the same neighborhood.

Many of the families attending Full Gospel

Tabernacle had moved to the suburbs and were driving back into the city for services. Dave realized his church had a big gymnasium and his congregation was largely middle-aged and older. The new church had mostly young people and children.

Dave approached the other pastor. "Look," he said, "you guys don't have a permanent facility. Why don't you come and use our gymnasium? You're short on mature Christians. We'll have our mature Christians help teach your Sunday School. We'll combine Sunday School, and have different worship services."

So they had two AG churches in one building—two churches with totally different styles. The newer church grew so much that the older church planted a new church in the suburbs and kept on growing.

You can go to just about any major street corner in America and see two, three, or sometimes four gas stations. That does not mean each station has less business. There is a synergy in multiple organizations pursuing a common goal. With the gas stations, consumers simply decide whether they want to buy Brand A, Brand B, or Brand C. They are happy to have the choice. In the same way, there is room for far more churches in America to create far more chances for people to choose Christ.

At Newport-Mesa Christian Center in Costa Mesa, when we hit five hundred people we outgrew our location and could not expand because of zoning restrictions. Planting a church was the natural solution. I brought a person on staff for six months to recruit as many people in our congregation as possible to plant a church in a neighboring community. About eighty people joined the effort, and we held a commissioning service on the last Sunday before we sent them out.

I asked the congregation, "How many of you have come to this church in the last six months and have made it your church home?" More than eighty people raised their hands. We had already replaced the people who were leaving.

I've heard this story countless times from other church planting pastors. Whether we want to believe it or not, the Scripture is true: "It is more blessed to give than to receive." The problem comes when we get into maintenance mode or status quo and are not pushing the envelope. Churches must have faith to continue to push the envelope for the next work God has in store.

Pastors need individual faith and congregations need corporate faith in constant pursuit of God's vision. The Lord has dreams and visions for the pastor and church who will take time to listen to His voice. The Holy Spirit certainly wants to reach our communities in America. If the Holy Spirit wants to reach our communities, then as we quiet ourselves and wait for His leading, He will show us what to do.

The Holy Spirit may not speak in an audible voice, but I've learned over the course of my life that the strong impressions that come in prayer are almost always from the Lord. I'll share one example.

When I left the campus pastorate at Evangel University, I was preaching to one thousand students a week. I was the first full-time campus pastor in the

Assemblies of God, I had just finished my doctoral work, and I intended to stay at Evangel the rest of my life.

In October 1970, just two months after completing my doctoral work, we had a Spiritual Emphasis Week. A great revival hit the campus. As I was praying, I looked across the students in chapel and I felt the Holy Spirit say to me, *George, look around here. This is not going to be your place of ministry much longer.*

I tried to write off the impression as a stray thought. I was prepared to serve there for the rest of my life. I found out months later that the church I would ultimately go to had set aside that last week of October as a week of prayer and fasting as they began to search for a new pastor. The Holy Spirit connected us.

In March 2007, I stood on the beach at Seleucia where Paul and Barnabas sailed from on their first missionary journey. As I stood on that beach, I had an incredible spiritual encounter. I realized at that moment that when Paul and Barnabas first set sail no book of the New Testament had been written, none of the Gentile churches had been founded except the church in Antioch, and Paul had no idea that in the next fifteen years he would plant churches in Antioch in Pisidia, Iconium, Lystra, Derbe, Philippi, Thessalonica, Berea, Athens, Corinth, and Ephesus. He had no hint of all the correspondence that would take place and form the New Testament. He could not see that Luke would come along as a partner and write Luke-Acts.

When Paul stood on the beach that day he knew none of that. As far as we know, he did not even have an itinerary. He had no five-year plan or ten-year plan. There is nothing wrong with such plans. But Paul had a sensitivity to the Spirit. He was willing to step out of the known, out of the great revival going on at Antioch. And that great church, where hundreds of people were coming to Christ, was sensitive to the voice of the Spirit and willing to give up its premier leaders in Paul and Barnabas.

Those missionaries literally did not know where they were going, except as the Spirit directed them. And the next fifteen years became an incredibly productive time for the Early Church.

I believe the Spirit wants to replicate that in our lifetime. He wants to take not only the young leaders anxious to get out and make a mark for God, but He also wants to take senior veterans and launch them into new ministries they never would have imagined. And as we partner with the Holy Spirit across this Fellowship, there are great churches in communities as yet unreached waiting to be born, waiting to impact their world for Christ.

May God burden our hearts and give us the vision for His great churches of the future.

SKILLFUL RESOURCING

WE CAN REACH

the WORLD

IF WE CAN

EQUIP

BELIEVERS

VISIT ANY ASSEMBLIES OF GOD CHURCH DUR-
ING A MISSIONS CONVENTION and you will
hear story after story of how a missionary's effectiveness on the field is directly proportionate to the
resources he or she receives from the network of supporting churches at home. The ill-equipped missionary
will struggle to establish a ministry. The well-equipped
missionary mobilizes local believers and over time sees a
chain of churches and Bible schools take shape.

Yes, there are spiritually resistant mission fields
where results are slim to none even with the best
resources and personnel in place. But as a rule, getting
the right gospel tools on-site in a timely fashion contributes to a bountiful spiritual harvest.

The same principle works domestically. In fact, I
would say the success of Assemblies of God World
Missions is not so much about churches underwriting
missions projects around the world, but rather it is
dependent on how those churches are established and
built up so those congregations in turn can share the
investment made in them.

Let's look at what is needed for a church to become
a productive partner in fulfilling the Great Commission.

OUR WORSHIP MUST CONNECT US WITH GOD

The most visible point of the local church is when the church meets for worship. I see some challenges our Fellowship needs to address in this very important aspect of church life. Much of what is called "worship" does little to connect the person in the pew with the Heavenly Father.

It does not promote intimacy with God, for example, when we robotically repeat choruses ad nauseum. I preach in many different churches and I notice from time to time the worship team is lost in its own world, eyes closed, oblivious to the congregation. I look around and hardly anyone in the congregation is even singing.

You have certainly heard reference to "worship wars" in our churches and the arguments for the relative merits of hymns and choruses. But so many new songs are being continually tried out, often with melodies that don't fit the words, that it is hard for a congregation to stay engaged. By the time they have learned a song, the worship team or worship leader has moved on, singing something totally different.

We used to have a unifying worship in the Assemblies of God. Our songs reflected our theology. I'm not saying we must go back to the old days at all; I realize we are far more diverse today than we were back then. But we must never abdicate our responsibility to worship in Spirit and in truth. If we think we must repeat a chorus often enough to induce people into some catatonic state where they will be worshipping in the heavens, then we have neglected worship with the mind as well as with the Spirit.

At churches that give an altar call, the music can be so deafening you cannot hear yourself pray. I was in an altar response at a church where the worship team took over. The drums were going, the guitars were going, the electric synthesizer was going—you could not pray if you wanted to because your sensory perceptions were overwhelmed with the music. When music is going on and people are trying to pray, the words and the music infiltrate their prayer and make it impossible for them to pray. Our culture has duped us into thinking there must always be music in the background.

I have started asking in many places where I minister that there be no music during the time at the altar. We need to hear God's people pray again. There is something wonderful about hearing the saints of God pray aloud within a worship context.

Since worship truly is to be our heartfelt communion with our God, it must reflect the best He has created within us. I am not saying we become so regimented that we do not let the Spirit move or give opportunity for His spontaneous gifts. But there must be excellence in what we do in concerted worship regardless of the size or makeup of our church. Recently, I visited a smaller church with about fourteen voices in the choir. They were absolutely fantastic. They had worked hard at their music; they did nothing slipshod. They offered the Lord the best they had.

THE WORD MUST BE
COMMUNICATED WITH LIFE

I can almost tell the spiritual health of the church by two things—the condition of the men's restroom and the condition of the pastor's library. Both tell you a lot about the church.

The men's room tells you whether or not there is a concern for detail. If any area of the building is going to be neglected, it is probably going to be that area. How in the world does that connect to a church's spiritual life? There is a correlation between how we care for things physically and how we care for things spiritually.

When I visit a pastor's library, I look to see if there are any good solid commentaries. As pastors, we have to feed our flock. If our only resource is Matthew Henry's *Commentary* from the sixteenth and seventeenth centuries, we're probably not going to speak relevantly to today's culture. A pastor must keep up to date.

Pastors must present the meat of the Word. Years ago I went into one pastor's library and there was only *Simple Simon Sermon Outlines* on his shelf. That was it—a little booklet called *Simple Simon Sermon Outlines* encased with cobwebs. I thought, *This is not going to be a good experience.* And it wasn't. Everything was as ragtag as you could imagine.

Giving your congregation spiritual nutrition does not require you to force-feed them everything at once. I think of one minister who preached twenty-minute sermons. He was a great preacher who communicated enormous life truth in those few minutes. But his preparation made that possible. He said he spent one hour in study for every minute he spent in the pulpit.

Most pastors cannot maintain that kind of schedule. They are counseling people, visiting people, and giving attention to the day-to-day details of the church. The pastor in a smaller church in particular does not have a staff to attend to those other responsibilities and can't think of spending twenty hours on one sermon. You have to find the right balance. I made it a practice as a pastor to spend about twenty hours a week in study for all the messages I had to prepare. If I did not study, I could not stay fresh.

The pastor who connects with his or her congregation must offer the Word with integrity and excellence. Just grabbing stuff off the Internet or lifting someone else's sermon from a commentary does not constitute resourcing the local church. To skillfully resource our people we must filter our studying through our life experience and what the Spirit is saying to us. The pastor is the primary Christian educator of the church—more than the Sunday School teacher, Royal Rangers or Girls Clubs leader, or Men's Ministries or Women's Ministries director. All of those ministries are important, but the pastor sets the bar. If he or she sets that bar high, there will be excellence throughout the system.

I look at the Internet much as I look at a library. It's a resource. To use it well as a resource and integrate what we learn off the Internet into our sermons contributes to the relevance and life of our presentation. To simply take stuff off wholesale is plagiarism. In the business world plagiarism is reason for termination. In the scholastic world plagiarism can terminate an academic career. We must be careful as ministers of the gospel that we have integrity. When we use someone else's material extensively we should give that person credit. At least say, "This comes from Pastor so-and-so, and it blessed my life, and so I've taken it, and I've massaged it, and I'm giving it to you." Failure in this discipline will short-circuit the whole internal process of study, prayer, and preparation in your own life for what God wants to do through you for your congregation.

As pastor I had a preaching plan of generally six months to a year out. I happen to be an expository preacher. When I was in seminary I remember reading an article in *Christianity Today* by W.A. Criswell, who was then marking his twenty-fifth anniversary as pastor at First Baptist in Dallas. He would serve over fifty years as pastor of that church. The article said that after twenty-five years he was just finishing with the Book of Revelation. He had begun preaching in Genesis when he became pastor and twenty-five years later he was finishing Revelation. Criswell attributed his connectivity in the church with his expository preaching.

God plans long-term. In the fullness of time, God sent His Son. How long did it take God to plan the Incarnation? It took awhile. He took time before Christ came in the fullness of time. It seems to me that as Pentecostals we think the Spirit only moves in spontaneous moments. The Spirit does move in spontaneous moments, but He also moves over the course of time. He can plan six months in advance as easily as He can plan one day in advance.

As a rule in my pastoral ministry, I had Sunday morning's sermon completed by Friday noon. I don't see how someone can minister effectively to a church by scrambling to prepare a sermon on Saturday night. Delivering sermons is like being pregnant. There's a gestation period that's needed. The message has to grow in your heart until it is ready to be delivered.

When I look at skillfully resourcing this Fellowship, the national office can do all the glitz stuff in the world to help the local church. But if that church is not skillfully resourced by its leadership, what the national offices do is irrelevant. Christian education, discipleship, and evangelism primarily take place at the local level.

THE PASTOR MUST UNDERSTAND THE CONGREGATION'S NEED

Sometimes we think, especially if ours is a smaller church, "When we grow we'll do better." Small churches grow into larger churches if they are thinking and preparing as if they were bigger. If you do things right when you are small, you will experience healthy growth.

Dr. Robert Frost, a leader in the charismatic renewal, began coming to our church with his wife, Ruth, when the church was small. Brother Frost prayed this prayer over me that I have mentioned earlier: "Lord, help them to lay foundations that are strong enough to bear the weight You will later place on them." That is part of skillfully resourcing the local church. We lay strong foundations. Whatever we do, we do with quality.

When our church had only sixty or seventy people, about two-thirds of our auditorium was empty. As I stated earlier, I prepared my sermons for an imaginary audience. I wanted a message to speak to a ten-year-old girl, to a high school junior or senior, to a young mother whose husband had just walked out on her, to a senior citizen who had just learned about ill health or had lost a spouse, to a college professor of comparative religions in the local university who decided to visit our church that morning with some students. I wanted my message to have validity for each of those people.

How could one message accomplish this? In reality, that is the case with every message we preach. A church is really a lot of people with different needs. But the Holy Spirit is able to take one message and distribute it in two hundred thousand different directions. Over the course of seventeen years every type of person in my imaginary audience became very real in my church.

As the Holy Spirit touched lives, it was amazing to me how often the Lord would bring a specific text to bear on an occasion in someone's life. I remember the Sunday I preached on the commandment "Honor your father and mother." I didn't know in planning that message that a truant girl who was running away from her parents would wind up in the congregation on that Sunday. The Lord used that message to bring that young woman to her parents and bring healing in that family.

I could never have known that the college professor who walked into the service one morning had psoriasis in his legs and that it was medically incurable and that his doctors had considered skin grafts and rejected the idea because it would grow right back. There I was preaching on Leviticus 13 and 14 saying, "Here, leprosy in the Hebrew doesn't just mean leprosy. It means eczema. It means psoriasis. It means any variety of skin disease." I went on to talk about what your skin is telling you about God. That professor and his wife accepted Christ and soon were baptized in the Spirit. They became two of the best lay workers we had in the church.

I could never have programmed any of that. Who in the world could have programmed that? That is the beauty of relying on God and committing ourselves to diligently prepare His Word to meet the needs of the flock He has entrusted to us.

DISTRICTS MUST OFFER
MORE THAN SEMINARS

We're in a process of transition in the Assemblies of God. The districts' primary function used to be to provide events, crisis management, and a credentialing process. This generation of ministers is looking for more than a surface functionary role for the district office. The districts' first priority must be to build relationships among their ministers. Directly related to that mission, districts must skillfully resource their churches.

I have served in office on a district level. I know the challenge departments at a district office face. In order to be well funded, they have to plan events that bring in revenue. The thinking goes something like this: *If X*

number of people show up for this retreat or this seminar,
and we meet budget, and we have something left over to
finance the department, we have had a successful year.

We must reconfigure our definition of success. Yes, districts can and should continue to offer events that draw churches and ministries together. There is nothing wrong with raising the funds necessary to support continued district ministry. But we need to retool what we offer at the district level so that we are able to say, "These Mpact Girls Clubs have been well resourced in our district. These Royal Rangers groups have been well resourced. These various components of the local church have been well resourced. These ministers have been well resourced."

Our picture of a successful district must change from how well the district is doing to how well the local churches are doing and how the district is helping those churches do well.

Here is what I hear often from younger ministers: "Why should we send our tithes to the district? We don't get any benefit from it." Sometimes such a statement is motivated by our narcissistic culture where we always want a bang for our own buck. I don't think any of us would be comfortable as pastors if our people started saying, "What am I getting out of my tithes?" But the truth is, people will quit tithing if we quit resourcing them. If our districts are going to continue to legitimately expect ministerial tithes, we have got to make sure we are doing our best to resource the people of God and to resource our ministers.

NATIONAL OFFICE DEPARTMENTS MUST BE CUTTING-EDGE

So in this whole subject of skillful resourcing, we make a mistake if we only question how the national office resources the local church. If national-level resourcing is to be effective, it must rest on a foundation of local church resourcing and district resourcing. But the fact remains that the Assemblies of God national office has a responsibility to this Fellowship. I see some wonderful avenues through which we are meeting this responsibility.

For example, we are skillfully resourcing this church through Assemblies of God Financial Solutions. The benefits to our ministers of having a great retirement plan they can contribute to, the benefits to our churches of having competitive loans available to them to finance church construction, the opportunity given to laypeople to strategically invest their resources in the kingdom of God both during and after their lifetime— all of these constitute a premier and skillful resource to this Fellowship.

Assemblies of God World Missions and Assemblies of God U.S. Missions are skillfully resourcing this Fellowship. There are no finer missions programs in the world. There are no finer videos and communications tools available to promote missions than you will find in this church. This is not something we use to boast or be prideful; every one of those resources is another reason to be grateful to God and to rejoice over the spiritual harvest He is giving to us.

We are skillfully resourced in our legal counsel. In the fourteen years I have been general secretary, the General Council has never lost a lawsuit. In fact, we have only been to trial one time, and that was a relatively minor case we won. When you compare that record with the Roman Catholic Church spending billions of dollars in payments to victims, you get a picture of how blessed we are.

This is largely the result of watchful care, another very important means of skillfully resourcing our churches. For example, we have repeatedly encouraged our churches to do background checks. Churches are learning they need Sunday School rooms with open doors or windows to see through. Classes should never place one adult with one child. Pastors need a see-through door into the office when counseling a member of the opposite sex. At the national level we do a criminal background check on all ministerial applicants. We're going to begin doing credit background checks for new applicants soon. These are all very important safeguards for the church. By making sure the right people get credentials, we are helping to protect the flock of God.

Since its establishment in 1994, the National Prayer Center has received millions of calls from people seeking help. At the central office, volunteers staff phones and share counsel and encouragement as they pray over people's needs.

An array of resources for the local church is being produced by various ministries in the national office. They are designed to assist churches and believers in sharing the timeless gospel while addressing today's changing needs.

Two innovative resources offered by Gospel Publishing House are producing incredible results. One of them, MEGA Sports Camp, was developed to teach soccer, basketball, baseball, and cheerleading skills alongside biblical truths. Since its beginning, more than twenty-five thousand kids have accepted Christ while attending a MEGA Sports Camp. The second resource, HighPoint, provides tools for an exciting, visitor-friendly children's program that teaches biblical character traits.

In spring 2008, the Evangelism Commission is releasing *Response Evangelism*, a seven-day devotional study designed to motivate and train believers for effective personal evangelism. This study is especially designed for the majority of church members who would not normally participate in a personal evangelism training course.

The Center for Church Leadership is launching a new Web site, MinistryDirect.com, to provide online resources, free sermon helps and downloads, and helpful polls to aid in local church ministry.

Already receiving a great response is the high-quality *Nothing's Too Hard for God* media campaign produced by the Office of Public Relations. Using eight true life stories, it emphasizes God's power to change lives.

At Gospel Publishing House we have three main product lines. Royal Rangers and Mpact Girls Clubs (formerly Missionettes) have gone through major product redevelopment in the past few years and are taking leader roles in the field. Our Radiant Life Sunday School curriculum has done well. There is a national downward trend in Sunday School that transcends the Assemblies of God, but our Sunday School figures are staying steady at one million in attendance. To improve in these areas, we are going to look to the practitioners—to our pastors, youth pastors, children's pastors, the people out in the field to help us.

We must be on the cutting edge not only of print resources but also of Internet and electronic resources. We are translating as many materials into major language groups as we can economically develop. Our national Center for the Blind is a premier leader for the blind. We're skillfully resourcing the body of Christ through ministries like Teen Challenge, MAPS RV'ers, institutional and military chaplains, and specialized ministries for youth, men, women, and children. And no matter how carefully I delineate our Fellowship's resourcing offices, I am sure to miss one. God has blessed us with an array of targeted resources any church would find useful.

This holds true for the people in our pews. There is a steadily growing demand for Christian products across our country. As just one example, I've asked GPH to look at what it can do to make sure we are giving proper recognition and promotion for our younger authors. We've got some great younger authors out there and we need to be relevant and current in publishing what they have to say.

LEADERSHIP MUST LISTEN IN ORDER TO EFFECTIVELY SERVE

It's critical our national leadership listen to our people. As much diversity as this church has, our leaders need to be listening to the many voices represented. From listening well we can offer resources and ministries well. I'll just cite one example.

The weeks leading up to the 2007 General Council saw a lot of Internet traffic on FutureAG.blogspot.com. I'm sure some of our older ministers looked a little askance at that, but when I looked at it, I had a positive reaction. This kind of forum is great. Our young people want to be part of this church. They are concerned about its future direction, and they want to have a hand in shaping it. In ten to thirty years, we older guys are going to be off the scene. The young ministers will be shaping the church in a way that textures it to where the Spirit is leading them.

I took time and I read the blog. I think I read everything on it, both before and after General Council, because I want to listen to what our younger voices, by and large, are saying. The blog started a poll on the candidates and posted questions for the candidates' response. I privately e-mailed one of the sponsors of the blog and explained I did not feel at liberty to respond to the questions because that forum had not yet been approved by the General Council itself in session.

That being said, the day of my election was Friday, August 10. It was a long day. I think I left the hotel room at 6:30 in the morning and got back at 1:30 the next morning. Back in my room, I couldn't get to sleep right away. I got on my computer and I felt impressed of the Spirit to go on the blog for the first time. I wanted to say to the younger people, "In this person, George Wood, you're going to have a friend who will listen to you. And I want you to know that right off the bat." My first official act as general superintendent was getting on the Internet and saying, "This is going to be a safe administration where you're going to be free to share without fear of threat or reprisal. We need to hear from you; we want to hear from you."

Relationship building and communication are vital to the current health and future vitality of this Fellowship. Will we be able to do everything everyone suggests we do? I would like to say yes, but I've already realized in this short time there are many different theories afloat as to which direction the Assemblies of God is going and what we should do next. But as our churches and ministers are encouraged to communicate, and as our leadership commits to maintaining a listening ear, we are going to be able to do a lot if we listen carefully and evaluate wisely.

My top prayer request is that God will give me and those serving with me on the leadership team wisdom. We cannot afford at this critical juncture in the life of the Assemblies of God to make mistakes or dumb decisions. And, of course, that has never been an option in our history. I'm reaching out to various groups. For example, I'm having the bloggers come in and talk with me to help me to engage the younger generation.

If we're going to know how to skillfully resource this Fellowship, we must skillfully listen first. As we listen, we must remember that two-thirds of the churches in this Movement are fewer than one hundred in attendance. One-third are fewer than fifty people on Sunday morning; one-third are between fifty and one hundred. I grew up in those churches. I understand those churches. And I have a deep love and respect for the pastors in those churches. They are the unsung heroes of the Assemblies of God. Many are bivocational, many are at very minimal levels of income, and many have no health insurance. Their families struggle, yet they are obeying the call of God. We need to be paying close attention as to how best to serve the small churches as well as the large churches.

ETHNIC REPRESENTATION MUST CONTINUE TO EXPAND

We must pay attention to how well we serve the nineteen and growing ethnic fellowships of the Assemblies of God. We know that 34 percent of our 2.8 million people in the U.S. Assemblies of God are from ethnic minorities. These groups are from around the world and represent another key aspect of our future.

I met with the leadership of a particular ethnic group which has fifteen or twenty of their churches as part of the Assemblies of God. That group has a total of six hundred churches throughout the United States. These are strong vibrant churches, and many of these churches are considering association with the Assemblies of God. They can be a great blessing to us. We have to ask ourselves how we can be a great blessing to them.

How can we skillfully resource every group represented in our Fellowship? The Commission on

Ethnicity, the various ethnic fellowships, our foreign language districts—these are all steps in the right direction. These ethnic and foreign language groups are a vital part of this Movement. They're not stepchildren, they are absolutely full-blooded brothers and sisters. We need to do whatever we can to skillfully resource them.

Then, as they bring their gifts alongside ours, the Assemblies of God will move into a new day of growth and effective ministry across this nation. And, yes, as this nation's churches are resources, we will count on many years to come of fruitful missions outreach around the world until our Lord returns.

FERVENT PRAYER

THE ASSEMBLIES

OF GOD'S

COMMITMENT

TO PRAYER

will DETERMINE

ITS DESTINY

PASSIONATELY PROCLAIM, STRATEGICALLY INVEST, VIGOROUSLY PLANT, SKILLFULLY RESOURCE—each of these elements is vital to the life and health of the Assemblies of God or of any church. But without a fifth core value, these first four will accomplish nothing. The church and the believer must fervently pray in order to accomplish anything for the Kingdom.

The Early Church father John Chrysostom expressed it most eloquently and succinctly: "God can refuse nothing to a praying church."

Harold Lindsell, former editor of *Christianity Today*, described the function of prayer this way:

> *God cannot do something unless we work. He stores the hills with marble, but He has never built a cathedral. He fills the mountains with iron ore, but He never makes a needle or a jet airplane. He leaves that to us.*

> *If then, God has left many things dependent on man's thinking and working, why should He not leave some things dependent upon man's praying? He has done so. 'Ask and you shall receive.' And there are some things God will not give us unless we ask.*

> *We cannot suppose that God will do for us* without *prayer what He has promised to do for us* only *through* prayer.

In Ephesians 6, Paul gives us a model of the Christian's spiritual armor. At the close of that section Paul offers this exhortation:

"And pray in the Spirit on all occasions with all kinds of prayers and requests. With this in mind, be alert and always keep on praying for all the saints.

"Pray also for me, that whenever I open my mouth, words may be given me so that I will fearlessly make known the mystery of the gospel, for which I am an ambassador in chains. Pray that I may declare it fearlessly, as I should" (Ephesians 6:18–20).

Take a look at those verses and all the references to prayer: "Pray ... prayers ... praying ... pray ... pray." Paul says we are to pray "on all occasions with all kinds of prayers and requests." At whatever point the other elements of the Christian's armor are in use, so too should be prayer.

Paul is saying that the shield and the breastplate and the helmet and the shoes are just standing there like an empty suit of armor in a museum unless the animating presence of prayer brings them to life. Without prayer we cannot accomplish the work of the Lord. It has been said countless times, but it is true: The church moves forward on its knees. If we are to see God work in our day and in our Fellowship, we must be praying people.

JESUS IS OUR EXAMPLE IN PRAYER

The term has almost become trite thanks to today's marketing machine: "What would Jesus do?" But I can assure you that whatever Jesus was doing during His earthly ministry, it was built on prayer. He regularly communed with His Father in order to accomplish His Father's mission.

Jesus never asked us to do something He himself did not do. Each of the Gospel writers shows us moments when Jesus was at prayer. Matthew notes nine such occasions, Mark, eight, Luke, thirteen, and John, five. Out of these thirty-five references, there are twenty-three separate occasions in Jesus' three-year ministry when the curtain is pulled back on details of Jesus' prayer life.

Study the life of Christ, and you will find Him praying at all the key moments. He prayed at His baptism. "As he was praying, heaven was opened."[1] He prayed prior to selection of the Twelve. "One of those days Jesus went out to a mountainside to pray, and spent the night praying to God."[2] When He faced rejection at Korazin, Bethsaida, Capernaum, Jesus prayed.[3] At Caesarea Philippi, prayer preceded one of Jesus' key revelations about himself. "Once when Jesus was praying in private and his disciples were with him, he asked them, 'Who do the crowds say I am?'"[4]

As you progress toward the end of Jesus' ministry, you continue to find Him in prayer. At His transfiguration, it is Jesus' prayer that brought about the key event. "About eight days after Jesus said this, he took Peter, John and James with him and went up onto a mountain to pray. As he was praying, the appearance of his face changed, and his clothes became bright as a flash of lightning."[5] At the grave of Lazarus, Jesus' prayer led to a miracle of resurrection.[6]

During the Passion Week, prayer was front and center in Jesus' life. At Passover, Jesus bathed the moment in prayer. "Then he took the cup, gave thanks, and offered it to them."[7] It was at this Passover that He prayed His high priestly prayer of John 17. In Gethsemane, Jesus prayed with every ounce of His strength. "And being in anguish, he prayed more earnestly, and his sweat was like drops of blood falling to the ground."[8] And we can never forget our Lord's prayers on the cross. "Father, forgive."[9] "Eloi, Eloi, lama sabachthani."[10] "Father, into your hands I commit my spirit."[11]

But, Jesus did not only pray at the key moments. He showed us that prayer must color all of our life. Jesus prayed when it was physically inconvenient. He prayed while it was still dark.[12] After an exhausting schedule culminating in the feeding of the five thousand, He went up to the hills to pray. When evening came, He was there alone.[13] On occasion, Jesus prayed all night long.[14]

And from these examples we discover there are many beneficiaries of Jesus' prayers. He prayed for others: for children, for disciples to receive the Spirit, for the faith of disciples to fail not. We learn Jesus set aside time and place for prayer. He withdrew to pray—seeking those times when He was least likely to be interrupted.

There is nothing half-baked about Jesus' prayers. He prayed with passion and intensity. "During the days of Jesus' life on earth, he offered up prayers and petitions with loud cries and tears to the one who could save him from death."[15]

Here's an astounding summary statement of Jesus'

main mission in the heavens as it relates to us, His people. Remember that the Old Testament high priest bore on his shoulders and his chest the stones symbolic of the twelve tribes of Israel. The weight of responsibility was on his shoulders, and their well-being was on his heart. Jesus, as our great High Priest, is gone into the heavens and the writer of Hebrews describes His mission there:

"Now there have been many of those priests, since death prevented them from continuing in office; but because Jesus lives forever, he has a permanent priesthood. Therefore he is able to save completely those who come to God through him, because he always lives to intercede for them" (Hebrews 7:23–25).

JESUS TAUGHT ON PRAYER

Not only did Jesus set the example in prayer, He taught continually regarding prayer, and His lessons in prayer can empower our prayer lives.

We are most familiar with Jesus' example prayer He taught the disciples. I like to call that prayer the "Disciple's Prayer," though it is more popularly known as the Lord's Prayer.[16] As we learn of prayer from Jesus, we find He taught us to pray for our enemies,[17] to pray privately rather than for show,[18] and to pray to the point, "Do not keep on babbling like the pagans."[19] In other words, stay engaged in your prayer. Don't go on automatic pilot.

Jesus taught us to persist in prayer—to ask, seek, and knock,[20] with the result being the gift of the Spirit. He gave us the example of the widow and the unjust judge[21] that we ought always to pray and not faint.

Jesus gave us worthy goals for our prayers. He told us to pray for workers in the harvest.[22] He told us some things cannot be done except through prayer.[23] He told us to pray in unity with others.[24] He told us to pray honestly and with humility.[25] He told us His house should be a house of prayer.[26]

Jesus instructed us to pray with faith. "Have faith in God....Therefore I tell you, whatever you ask for in prayer, believe that you have received it, and it will be yours."[27] He told us to pray with forgiveness[28] and personal integrity.[29] We are to pray to avoid temptation.[30]

We are to pray in Jesus' name.[31]

JESUS WARNED AGAINST NEGLECTING PRAYER

Mark 9:14–29 gives us one of the most direct warnings in Scripture against neglecting prayer. Jesus had come down from the Mount of Transfiguration after showing His glory to Peter, James, and John. When He and the three disciples came down, the other nine disciples who had been left behind were in a big argument. There was a large crowd around them, and they were arguing with the teachers of the law.

The first lesson I see in this passage cuts to the heart of church life. When the church has no power, it is reduced to argument.

Jesus came upon this scene and learned what all the hubbub was about. A man had brought his demon-possessed son to the disciples for deliverance. Now the man himself came forward, presented his son, and described his son's condition. It was horrific. The boy could not speak and would wildly try to harm himself.

I see a second lesson here. What happened to that boy is an example of what the devil tries to do with lives. Whether or not a person is demon-possessed, this is what the devil is trying to do. He is trying to rob us of our speech so we can't articulate clearly who we are in God's eyes. He is seizing us and throwing us down. He never pulls us up; he never builds us up; he never lifts us up.

Jesus, confronted with this need, was angered at the temporary victory Satan was winning. There was, as yet, no spiritual strength being applied against the demonic manifestation. Jesus' next words were harsh and evidently aimed at the disciples—though He may have been also addressing the crowd. "O unbelieving generation," Jesus replied, "how long shall I stay with you? How long shall I put up with you?" (Mark 9:19).

By this time, Jesus had been with the disciples more than two years. Mark 6 records how they had been given power to go out and cast out demons and they did exactly that (Mark 6:8-13). "They drove out many demons and anointed many sick people with oil and healed them." They had experienced powerful ministry success already, but this problem proved too hard with them. What had happened?

Jesus came right to the point. The disciples were struggling with unbelief and powerlessness. Why were they unbelieving and why were they powerless? Jesus identified the cause: "This kind can come out only by prayer" (Mark 9:29). While some versions include fasting in the text, Jesus' first focus was prayer. He directed the disciples' attention to their prayerlessness and that their prayerlessness had resulted in powerlessness.

A church that does not fervently pray is not going to see God moving in its midst. That congregation may limp along doing a few things in its own power, but it isn't going to accomplish much. If the Assemblies of God is to effectively reach this world, then prayer must become the foundational characteristic of our Fellowship.

THE LIFE OF A CHURCH IS PRAYER

I believe every service in an Assemblies of God church should give opportunity for people to be prayed for. That should be true without exception. At any time a person with the direst need may walk through the door. I'll give an illustration.

Two of my very closest life friends were going through a grave emergency. Their son was in the midst of a divorce, battling for child custody and became very depressed. The man was suicidal. My friends flew just to be with him, and they asked me for a church in his community where they could connect. I gave them the name of a really good growing Assemblies of God church.

They visited the church and asked the greeter, "Is there someone we could have pray with us?" They were told, "Here's a card. Fill this out." In the service there was no invitation given for anyone who had need for prayer. On their way out, they contacted another person. "We have a desperate situation," they said. "Could someone pray with us?" "If you could e-mail that prayer request into us," they were told, "we pray for the requests that are handed in or mailed in during the week."

My friends had made, in the course of that one Sunday morning, three attempts to be prayed with. "We were so desperate," they told me later, "and we feel so badly."

I felt badly because I had recommended the church.

Fortunately, my friends clung to the truth that God hears and answers prayer. They had been reading in Kings about two situations. In one, Jehu only halfheartedly rid the land of the idolatrous high places (2 Kings 10). In the second, Jehoash, in response to Elisha's command, only halfheartedly struck the ground with arrows when commanded to hit the ground as a symbol of victory over God's enemies (2 Kings 13). My friends sensed God was saying to them, "What are you halfhearted about? Your victory requires tenacity!" They determined to "strike the ground" again and again with their prayers. And, ultimately, their prayers were answered.

Jess Moody wrote a book years ago called *The Drink at Joel's Place*. Moody said a church must be what it advertises. Most churches are saying to their community in one way or another, "Here is a community of people of faith, here's a community of people who pray, here's a community of people of God, here's a community that loves one another, here's a community that has joy."

If the church doesn't practice those things, it can wear an Assemblies of God name or whatever name it wants, but it's the reality of what is going on inside that community of believers that will prove the worth and vitality of that church to the community. And prayer is the key to a church's delivering on its promises. There should not be a service in an Assemblies of God church where there is not fervent prayer.

I have had the privilege of preaching at Cornerstone Church in Bowie, Maryland, pastored by Mark Lehmann. I believe they have one of the finest weekly prayer meetings in our Fellowship.

Every Saturday evening a substantial number of Cornerstone's congregation gathers for prayer in the sanctuary. Those prayer gatherings have been a mainstay of that church's life for more than ten years. Each Saturday evening, scores of congregation members walk between the pews, praying for God to work in hearts and meet the needs of those who will sit there the next day.

The certificates and photos of the missionaries Cornerstone supports are not in the lobby, but are framed and hang on the walls of the church sanctuary. Congregation members can be seen around the walls praying fervently for the missionaries pictured. Prayer is part of the fabric and DNA of that church. We need many more of our congregations to take prayer that seriously.

Early in my years as a pastor, a gentleman by the name of Armin Gesswein would periodically visit our church. He was an older gentleman who in the early days of Billy Graham's ministry had been a prayer counselor to Billy Graham. Armin was a wonderful man of prayer.

"George," he said to me, "I visit and minister in a lot of churches. One of the things I look at in church bulletins is whether there are any prayer meetings taking place."

I pondered that.

"I'm afraid to say," he continued, "that in a lot of churches there are many events, but there's little publication of when the church is meeting for prayer."

When he was done talking to me, I immediately grabbed my bulletin from that day just to check, and I was only partially reassured. While we did have prayer meetings announced, there were not enough. I began to make prayer a greater priority for our church.

I went to Newport Christian Center in 1971. We merged in 1973 with First Assembly of God in Costa Mesa, to form Newport-Mesa Christian Center. First Assembly had a larger facility, double the size of Costa Mesa's church. Having gone through a terrible church split, First Assembly's attendance was down to about sixty people, and the bank was close to foreclosing on the property.

Wayne and Diane Tesch served as associates with me for sixteen of my seventeen years in Costa Mesa, and we went into that sanctuary before our congregation moved and spent several hours in prayer. We went to each door, anointed it with oil, and prayed that all who entered and exited would experience the peace of God and the work of the Spirit, and that He would protect the congregation from division. We were in that church for seven years, from 1973 to 1980.

I continued to encourage our people in prayer throughout my pastorate, and when I was preparing to leave Newport-Mesa Christian Center I could identify some 95 percent of the congregation who had come into the church during my time as senior pastor as a result of prayer-bathed growth.

As I contemplated the pastoral search in which the church would soon be engaged, I also remembered my recent observation of another church seeking a pastor. The primary requirement was that he had an earned doctorate. That church did not approach the search prayerfully seeking the Lord's help; rather, they simply poured over résumés. They ended up calling a pastor who had earned two doctorates; it was a disaster. The man had a moral failure and many people ended up leaving the church. I wanted to ensure that would not happen at Newport-Mesa.

I called the church to a twenty-four hours a day, seven days a week time of prayer in which congregation members signed up for fifteen-minute blocks of time throughout the day and night, until the Lord so clearly sent Pastor Jim Bradford to be their pastor. He had a wonderfully effective pastorate at Newport-Mesa for twelve years. I am thoroughly convinced prayer was the primary factor in God bringing Jim Bradford to that pastoral assignment.

It is too easy for us to rely on our own efforts and our own strength. Prayer drives us to our knees in dependence upon God, reminding us that human effort cannot accomplish His purposes.

PRAYER WILL MAXIMIZE THE CHURCH'S MINISTRY

When I was a young minister, I called on E.S. Williams, general superintendent of the Assemblies of God from 1929 to 1949. He was at Maranatha Village, the

Assemblies of God retirement community in Springfield, Missouri. He was in his early nineties.

Brother Williams was a great man of God who had led this Movement so well. I had a special relationship with him because my mother studied under E.S. Williams in Bible school some years before he became general superintendent. My wife, Jewel, and I wanted to visit Brother Williams and have him pray a blessing over our ministry.

In the course of that conversation and prayer, I said to him, "Brother Williams, you've been with the Assemblies of God practically since the beginning." (He was a product of the Azusa Street Revival.) "What's your greatest concern for the Assemblies of God?"

He was so quick and sharp even in his last years. Without batting an eye he said, "Socialization." He explained what he meant. As people get saved and their families get saved and their friends get saved, they enjoy one another's company. They're glad to be out of the world, and if they are not careful they can allow church to become just another social club of nice people and forget their mission as a church.

I never forgot that. Why does the church exist? To reach a spiritually dead world with the life-giving gospel. Prayer will keep us from forgetting our mission. Prayer will remind us of our dependence upon the Lord to carry out that mission. Powerlessness is a direct result of prayerlessness.

When I spoke for Sister Berniece Hicks and the Christ Gospel International Church in Jeffersonville,

Indiana, I walked into their 6 pm prayer meeting leading into their 7 pm Sunday evening service. I thought I had gone back to the days of my childhood in the Assemblies of God.

Everyone was praying aloud. There was no background music drowning out the prayer; it was just prayer. It was a fervent calling out to God. There was weeping, there were silent voices, there were loud voices, there were young and old, people were kneeling, people were standing, people were laying prostrate on the ground. They were just fervently calling out to God.

No wonder that local church has planted two thousand churches worldwide! Those are people of fervent prayer. They don't have super ability in themselves. They have an eighty-nine-year-old pastor who is a woman of prayer, and they have been taught to pray. With prayer, they have developed a supernatural ability to multiply the Kingdom around the world.

I think of another elderly saint of God leading a dynamic AG congregation. Way of Faith Assembly of God in Fairfax, Virginia, is thriving under the leadership of Rev. Ellen Blackwell. Sister Blackwell was ninety-three when I had the privilege in May 2007 of dedicating facilities overlooking the Sea of Galilee in Israel. Sister Blackwell and Way of Faith built that one million dollar facility through prayer in order to make a house of prayer available to their people and the body of Christ. Sister Blackwell is going as strong as if she were in her sixties. She spends hours daily in prayer, and prayer has made her a true Caleb who is not afraid, at her advanced age, to take the next mountain for God!

That is the dynamic we must have across the Assemblies of God if we are going to be effective for the Lord. We must be people of prayer.

Serving at our national office, I am even more convinced our national offices must set an example for our churches. We begin too many meetings with perfunctory prayer. Anyone who thinks it is a courtesy to God to open a meeting with prayer does not grasp just how vital God's leading is in our business matters. We must passionately pray for His guidance.

Our chapel services at the national office need the same evaluation. I want to make our prayer time as a corporate headquarters body more meaningful. I want to see us take the initiative to pray for one another. I want people to feel free to come forward as the Spirit leads them and offer prayers. I want to see our prayer time be more extended. We need to recover the sense of what it means for the people of God to pray together. The Early Church devoted itself to the apostles' doctrine, to breaking of bread, and to prayer. We must do the same thing.

Our National Prayer Center is another vital aspect of prayer ministry at the national office. Currently, the number of incoming calls is overwhelming the phone system. We are making provision technologically to handle more, but NPC Director John Maempa informed me we need at least 250 additional part-time people to man the phones. I am instructing all department heads at our national office to request our employees to each take a half hour per week to be on the phones to pray with people who call into the NPC. For a Pentecostal organization that believes in and depends on the Holy Spirit to move, it is essential we be people of prayer.

PRAYER WILL EMPOWER THE BELIEVER IN GOD'S SERVICE

I was talking with a couple of missionaries who work in a very difficult area of the world where their lives are in constant danger because of their mission for Christ. They told me that they pray with their ministry team every morning for two hours. "It's a matter of life and death," they said.

Whether or not we realize it, the mission of the local church and of every believer in the church is also a matter of life and death. Even in the absence of persecution, there are people around us in desperate need of a saving gospel that can preserve them from eternal separation from God. Prayer makes a life-or-death difference in eternal souls. That is where the need to pray fervently comes into clearest focus. Prayer in the context of the church's saving mission is not perfunctory. It is a necessity, and souls are at stake.

It was February 9, 1958, and a young Assemblies of God pastor in rural Pennsylvania was watching "The Late Show" on TV while his wife and small children were asleep. A few years earlier, this young pastor had been in the carpool with my sister riding from Pittsburgh to Central Bible Institute in Springfield, Missouri. As a student, he had wanted to preach in my dad's church; but even though Dad's church only had about thirty or forty people, Dad thought this young skinny kid had not yet had enough experience to preach in Dad's "big church."

A few years had gone by, and this young man's small rural church had grown from 50 to 250—his first pastorate. That February night he evaluated his life. "How much time am I spending in front of the TV each night?" he asked himself. "A couple of hours at least. What if I sold the TV set and spent that time praying?"

Next morning he and his wife agreed to sell the TV if after putting the ad in the paper it sold within half an hour after the paper hit the streets. At the twenty-ninth minute, the phone rang. "How much?" The young pastor had not even thought of the price. He blurted out, "one hundred dollars." The caller said, "I'll take it. I'll be there in fifteen minutes."

On February 25, a late Tuesday evening near the end of his prayer time—just two weeks and two days after the decision to sell the TV—this young pastor was in his study praying, and began to feel a great heaviness. He felt an urge to pick up *Life* magazine, but resisted at first because he didn't want to fall into a trap of reading a magazine during his prayer time. He had been fidgeting that evening—his wife and children had been away visiting grandparents in Pittsburgh. The magazine beckoned to him from his desktop. Finally, he said, "Lord, is there something You want me to see?" He sat down in his brown swivel chair and opened the magazine.

He leafed through it and came to a page that at first seemed to have nothing to interest him. It carried a pen drawing of a trial taking place 350 miles away in New

York City—a place he had never been. His attention was caught by the eyes of the figure in the drawing, a boy, one of seven on trial for murder. The look in the boy's eyes was one of bewilderment, hatred, and despair. The young pastor began to cry. He said aloud to himself, "What's the matter with me?"

He looked at the picture more carefully. The boys were all teenagers. They were members of a gang called the Dragons. They had brutally attacked and killed a fifteen-year-old polio victim named Michael Farmer. The seven boys had stabbed Michael in the back seven times with their knives, then beat him over the head with garrison belts. They went away wiping blood through their hair, saying, "We messed him good."

The story revolted the young pastor. It turned his stomach. Then a thought came, "Go to New York City and help those boys." On Friday morning, the young pastor was in the courtroom—and the rest is history. Had David Wilkerson not given himself to prayer, Teen Challenge would never have happened.

A needlepoint in David Wilkerson's office is from his daughter, Bonnie: *My dad is famous not for who he is, but because he dared to listen when God wanted to hold conversation.*

That is what prayer is in its simplest definition—a conversation with God. And yet we too easily gloss over what is embodied in that definition. We are given the immeasurable privilege of coming into the intimate presence of our Heavenly Father and communing with Him. When we remember the price He paid in order to make that relationship possible, it should give us a clue as to how deeply He desires our fellowship.

God's Son died and shed His blood to atone for the sins that would otherwise separate us from the Father. Throughout His earthly life, Jesus had shown His disciples and a watching world just what could be accomplished through undiluted intimacy with the Father. Then He laid everything on the line to make such a relationship available to all of us.

Are we truly ready to fulfill Christ's Great Commission in this world? We can only do so by following His example and His teaching on prayer. Jesus himself passionately proclaimed the gospel, strategically invested in His disciples, vigorously planted the seeds of His church, and skillfully resourced those who would bring that Church into reality. But He did all of it on the strength of fervent prayer.

We can do no less.

[1]Luke 3:21; [2]Luke 6:12; [3]Matthew 11:25,26; [4]Luke 9:18; [5]Luke 9:28,29; [6]John 11:41,42; [7]Matthew 26:27; [8]Luke 22:44; [9]Luke 23:34; [10]Mark 15:34; [11]Luke 23:46; [12]Mark 1:35; [13]Matthew 14:23; [14]Luke 6:12; [15]Hebrews 5:7; [16]Matthew 6:9-13; [17]Matthew 5:44; [18]Matthew 6:5-8; [19]Matthew 6:7; [20]Luke 11:9-13; [21]Luke 18:1-8; [22]Matthew 9:38; [23]Mark 9:29; [24]Matthew 18:19,20; [25]Luke 18:9-14; [26]Mark 11:17; Luke 19:46; [27]Mark 11:22-26; [28]Mark 11:25; [29]Mark 12:40; [30]Luke 22:40; [31]John 14:13,14; 15:7; 16:23-26

[ACTION PLAN]

T O BENEFIT FROM DR. WOOD'S INSIGHTS AND CHALLENGES, thoughtfully consider your ministry and local church:

+ Is God increasing your desire to see the lost come to Christ? How are you sharing the message of Jesus in your everyday life?

+ If you are a pastor or church leader, in what ways can you lead your congregation into more effective evangelism in your community?

+ In what ways can you devote time to mentor a young person whom the Lord has placed in your life?

+ How can you and your church be more proactive in investing in the next generation?

+ How strong is your church's vision to plant a church or partner with others to do so?

+ In what areas could your congregation use additional resources?

+ How can you increase the quality of your personal prayer life and that of your congregation?